# The Midlife Launch:

Successfully Pursue Your Dream Without Giving Up What's Most Important to You

KINGSLEY GRANT

Copyright © 2016 Kingsley Grant

All rights reserved.

ISBN: 0988414236

ISBN-13: 9780988414235

# DEDICATION

This book is dedicated to all those who are in the midlife stage of life thinking that their best years are behind them. They are afraid to try new things and go after the dream that is burning a hole within their heart. They know they should be doing something else other than that which they are currently doing but are afraid. They are imagining the worse ... the loss of relationships and other resources. Taking a risk at this stage of life is frightening.

Here's to you. It's never too late. The time is NOW! Pursue your midlife dream life!!!

# ACKNOWLEDGMENTS

This book has been a work in progress. It has not been easy to finally make the decision to publish it. I had to work through a number of limiting beliefs, some of which I describe in the book, but I could not have done this without the support of my family – my wife and children. They allowed me time to myself to write, research and engage with other like-minded people. I also want to acknowledge my many coaches and mentors who have been invaluable in this journey. Most importantly, I want to acknowledge My God and Savior – Jesus Christ – for the wisdom, insights and the mind overhaul to do what I do. He has poured so much peace, love and joy into me, that sustains me each and every day.

# TABLE OF CONTENTS

DEDICATION ................................................................................. i

ACKNOWLEDGMENTS ............................................................... iii

INTRODUCTION ........................................................................... 1

THE DAY IT ALL BEGAN ............................................................. 8

THE VALLEYS AND THE MOUNTAINS ................................... 16

FEAR CAN BE A FOE OF YOUR MIDLIFE LAUNCH .............. 24

FAMILY CAN BE FOES OF YOUR MIDLIFE LAUNCH .......... 42

FRIENDS CAN BE FOES OF YOUR MIDLIFE LAUNCH ......... 56

THE RESPONSIBILITY CARD ..................................................... 65

TAPPING INTO YOUR LIFE'S EXPERIENCE ............................ 82

YOUR NETWORK - YOUR NETWORTH ................................. 100

ROB THE GRAVEYARD OF ANY FUTURE RICHES ............. 114

TAKING THE PLUNGE ............................................................... 134

ABOUT THE AUTHOR ............................................................... 149

BIBLIOGRAPHY .......................................................................... 152

# INTRODUCTION

✓ Do you have a burning desire to live the life that you've always wanted?

✓ Are you feeling comfortably miserable with where you are and what you are doing right now?

✓ Are you feeling restless in your current place of employment because you are just going through the motions knowing there is more you could be doing with your life?

✓ Is being location independent a dream of yours?

✓ Do you want to more freedom and flexibility in your life?

If your answer to most or all of the above questions is yes, keep on reading. This book is designed with you in mind.

The MIDLIFE LAUNCH is simply making the case that at this stage of life, you are more equipped now to go after and succeed at pursuing your dream, than at any other time in your life.

Psychologist Erik Erikson refers to this stage of life as The Midlife Stage. According to his explanation it is comprised of the years that span from 40 to 64 years of age.

He also labels this stage of life as a period of stagnation.

Stagnation according to Erickson, is when a person reaches the point in their life when they are trying to figure out who they are. "Midlifers" ask the questions, "Who am I without the labels of dad, boss, president, supervisor, manager, lawyer, etc?"

We begin an identity search at this stage, very similar to our identity search during the adolescence stage of life. However, this time, we are redefining ourselves.

There is a sense of confusion and uncertainty as to what to do at this point. Erikson suggests that the question being subconsciously (or consciously) asked is "Can I make my life count?" This question is centered on work and parenthood, even though there are other areas in which we define ourselves.

That's where I was – this state of indecision during the process of reinventing myself – in the latter part of 2007 and the early part of 2008.

I entered what would be considered "midlife." I began to look closely at my life to see if there were any areas of significance – any areas that mattered. I, like everyone else who enters this stage, was examining under a mental microscope what I had accomplished so far.

I was also speculating on the likelihood of me accomplishing anything more in my lifetime. This brought on great discontent and some moments of depression. I realized I had to do something if I was going to change it and it had to be done quickly.

The discontent brought on the idea of either changing my career and getting another J.O.B or launch out into the ocean of my dream. I chose the latter.

Here are the six reasons why I chose the latter and why I think it would be in your best interest to do the same. These were some of my underlying motives:

1. **Being in control:** taking control of my life and being responsible for my destiny. This is one of the unique aspects of the Midlife Launch. The Midlife Launch removes the idea of someone else dictating how, when and where you do life. It empowers you and makes you responsible for your own destiny rather than someone else.

2. **Doing what I love:** I think it was Confucius who said, "find a job you love and you never have to work another day in your life." To me that sums up this second reason. As a part of the Midlife Launch, I realize that I was going to be doing what I loved. Instead of putting all my energy and hours into someone else's dream, I was going to be putting it into my own endeavor.

3. **Having Financial Freedom:** Instead of making someone else "rich" through my effort and sweat, why not make myself "rich" (rich in having a more fulfilled life)? Why not work the

40 to 60 hours a week doing my own thing – pursuing my own dream and doing what I love?

4. **Being location flexible:** The thought of setting up my business in such a way that could give me location independence, was hard to dismiss. Think about it for a moment: that means I could have my business without being "tied" to a building. As a matter of fact, I would advise you not to invest in buildings – such as buying or renting office space – unless it is a real estate investment. Why not consider working out of your home, the library or a coffee shop? I've done all of the above.

5. **Having unlimited access to whoever would welcome my invitation to connect:** We are living in a time when the information age has allowed us to virtually do business from almost anywhere in the world. All we need is a computer and Wi-Fi. The world is linked together, which gives us access to billions of people. Social media makes it quite easy to be in contact with anyone and everyone, so we don't have any excuses. The gatekeepers who once were able to selectively determine who had access to what and where are no longer able to prevent you from gaining access. They can't stop you.

6. **Choosing my best Midlife now:** It is never too late to live your best life now – have the most fulfillment now, have the most pleasure and joy, even have the most comforts now. At

midlife, you have a chance to do a lot of things over – you can start fresh. Why not do it now? If not now, then when are you going to pursue your dreams? Remember time is of the essence. Whether you do something or not, time still marches on. Tomorrow will come and go so why not invest your time in taking actions that will create a more fulfilling and meaningful life now and for the future?

These were just some of the reasons I chose to turn my passion into a profitable lifestyle business. It gave me the freedom and flexibility that I was looking for or at least it promised me that. It is not an overnight destination. It takes patience and lots of hard work but at least I'm doing something that I love doing.

Here's what I know about you.

You have accumulated incredible experiences - the good, the bad and the ugly, which all can now serve you in more ways than you can imagine. You'll see how this translates as you continue to read this book.

Whether you are aware of it or not, you are dealing with issues in life that are unique to this stage of life. No other stages - adolescence, young adult or the elderly stage - have the kind of stressors and responsibilities as you do. You are smack-dab in the middle of the stressors. You are as someone has said, "between a rock and a hard place."

Connecting with your purpose and following after your passion, living a life of significance, doing what you want to do in life and building future financial security is more important now than at any other time in your life.

Standing in the way of living the life you want, are the demands being placed upon you. These are added stress, that you feel overwhelmed by. You are now thinking of the present and future - retirement, aging parents, adult children, grand-children, savings, health and the list continues. All these create a "rock and a hard place" feeling.

You are also asking the circular questions that you may have directly or indirectly asked during your adolescent years: Who am I? Why am I here?

In addition, you may be looking at your life and assessing your accomplishments. Not seeing what you thought you would be doing at this point in your life, you feel the added stress of that; you're feeling the "I'm running out of time" pressure.

This book is designed to normalize some of those feelings. It highlights some of the experiences of people who are or were just like you and provides you with some practical ideas of what to do in these situations.

The one theme you will find throughout this book is the simple message - "Don't let your dream die within you."

My mother did.

# THE MIDLIFE CHALLENGE

## Chapter 1

## THE DAY IT ALL BEGAN

It happened on January 1, 2011. I remember that day like it was yesterday. At six o'clock in the morning the phone rang. Our home phone doesn't normally ring that early. As a matter of fact, we almost exclusively use our cell phones. Usually, when the house phone rings it means a telemarketer is calling.

However, my mom, who lived in Jamaica, was very ill. Most of the calls that are made from Jamaica are made via a land line because they are more economical than cell phones. Instead of ignoring the ringing, I rolled over and reached for the noisy intruder.

The phone was within reach. It nestled on the nightstand beside my bed. It was in an upright position within its base. I was able to see the display screen from where I laid. I strategically placed the phone this way so that I could easily glance on the screen and determine whether or not I should answer or let the voice mail take the call.

Groggy as I was and making a valiant effort to focus, I recognized the area code as that of Jamaica. The three digits that stared at me were 876. This is the international area code for Jamaica. I immediately knew this might be a call I should answer. I made out the other digits and recognized that it was that of my sister who also lives in Jamaica.

My mind raced as I tried to imagine what this call was about. Why would my sister be calling so early? I thought of two things. She was calling to tell me that my mom had been released from the hospital or that she didn't make it out of the hospital.

This all happened so quickly.

I dismissed the first thought because my sister whose name is Charmaine, could have relayed that message at a more convenient time during the day. Calling so early was risky ... she risked me getting angry at her; not that I do or would have done that, but it was a risk.

I picked up the phone and said "hello" in as sleepy a voice as I could muster; one that said, don't be long, I want to go back to sleep.

"Good morning Jay," came the voice on the other side. (Jay is my nickname that my family and others who grew up with me, use.) It was Charmaine's voice. Recognizing her low tone, I knew something was wrong. I feared for what I would hear next.

It was almost two weeks since I had visited my mom in Jamaica.

I had spent a week visiting with her in the hospital. She had her up and down days, but the general trend of her health was very much down. I would talk to her as much as possible while she listened, or I would just sit by her bedside while she rested. Even though she was so sick, I could always count on her to smile. When I looked at her face it was hard to gauge how much pain she was in.

When it was time for me to return to the United States I prayed with her, something that I did every evening before I left the hospital to return to my sister's home. However, this prayer was different.

I realized I might not see her again on this side of eternity. I choked up and held back the tears because I didn't want to add more stress to her by crying. I took several deep breaths and then kissed her forehead as she laid on the bed. She smiled at me and said in parting, "God bless you my son. I love you."

I hoarsely whispered, "I love you too mom," as I closed the mesh that surrounded her bed keeping the mosquitos and flies away. Because of the conditions of the hospital we had to provide a mosquito net to allow her to sleep without being pestered by pesky mosquitoes and flies. I tied the enclosure as securely as I could, took another deep breath, and walked away with tears filling my eyes.

I felt as if I had held that deep inhalation of breath that I took inside the hospital until I walked outside into the fresh air. At this point, I pushed out that breath as hard as I could. My mind was racing. "Would I see my mom again?"

I sat in the car for a few minutes and gathered my thoughts. I started the engine, opened the windows, and drove off into the night. The next day, I boarded a plane and returned to the United States. Something within me gave me that eerie feeling that I probably would not see her again. I had my time with her. I took care of any unfinished business I might have had. I said my "goodbye" and was at peace with myself, her and God.

So when the phone rang and I heard my sister's voice, I responded, "Hey Charm, what's up?"

I waited as I could hear her trying to keep her voice from cracking. When she was able to speak again, it was in an even softer voice: "Mom passed."

Silence.

It seemed like an eternity passed before I could say anything again. "Hmmm," I replied – that was all. I'm not sure if that was because I was in shock or because I was anticipating this call.

Another moment of silence passed, and then, to keep the conversation short, I thanked her for the call, uttered "Wow" and "I'll talk with you later" then hung up the phone.

By this time my wife was fully awake. The phone's insistent rings had disturbed her sleep as well. We normally would have slept for another hour or so, especially seeing it was New Year's Day..

"What happened honey," she asked very suspiciously.

"Mom has died," I uttered without looking towards her. I was on my back in a meditative mode.

"Oh no. Sorry honey" she said as she reached over and put her hands across my chest.

We hugged and just laid there in silence.

That is how I began my new year of 2011.

Mom's death brought me back to a conversation that I had a few weeks earlier with my sister - Charmaine. We were reminiscing about our childhood and growing into adulthood. As we discussed our goals for the future, we somehow got onto the topic of mom and her life career.

Mom was a schoolteacher all of her adult life. All she had ever done was teach.

She loved teaching. She was a very dedicated teacher. At the school that she spent most of her years teaching, a library was built and named in her honor.

My sister proceeded to tell me that she had asked mom about what else she would have done if she had not become a teacher. "A nurse", was my mom's immediate reply. She had always wanted to be a nurse!

My mom died with that nurse inside of her. That nurse will never have the opportunity to make a difference in someone's life.

Here's the message for you: Don't let another nurse, a musician, or writer die within you!

This puts me in mind of something one of my favorite speakers – Dr. Myles Monroe – once said. I heard him one day share with a group of college graduates that a graveyard is one of the wealthiest places on earth. He explained that a graveyard was wealthy because there are people who were buried there with songs in them that were never sung, books that were never written, businesses that were never started, cures for certain diseases that were never developed, and on and on he went. He did not need to say more. I got the message.

I decided that I did not want to add to the riches of any graveyard. I realized that I had something in me that I wanted to get out. I wanted to live what I considered to be the best life I could live ... now. I wanted to have my own business, which I have since done. I wanted to be an author, and I have since written several books. I wanted to become a better speaker so that I could inspire hope in others; I have since given a number of speeches while learning the finer art of speaking through Toastmasters International.

I want to die having emptied myself of all that God has placed in me.

Has it been easy? Certainly not!

Has it been worth it? More than definitely!

What about you? Do you want to enrich a graveyard or live your life to the fullest? I know this is somewhat of a morbid conversation to have especially to begin this book, but I believe it's one that we must have and not shy away from.

In the words of Steve Jobs to Steve Scully, who was the CEO of PepsiCo at the time, and was being recruited by Steve to join Apple: "Do you want to spend the rest of your life selling sugared water or do you want to change the world?"

You change the world through living your dream.

Are you living your dream or are you selling sugared water?

# Chapter 2

# THE VALLEYS AND THE MOUNTAINS

So, what is your dream; your passion?

Because you are reading this book, it tells me that you have a dream deep inside of you: you want to live the life you've always wanted.

You want to be the master of your own destiny, the servant to none.

You want autonomy - the freedom to do the work you love and the flexibility to go where you want, when you want and to financially support this lifestyle.

You have had enough of making others wealthy while leaving your dream at the door. You now want to pursue your passion and find a way to turn it into a profitable endeavor and create a more positive outlook on your financial future.

How do you picture your dream?

Do you want to open your own restaurant, be the chef, and have a personal relationship with your customers? Have you always wanted to own an eclectic coffee shop that is the heart of your small town? Have you dreamed of being a writer, a public speaker or a coach? What about a consultant?

Your dream may look very different from the next person's dream. In fact, your dream probably looks very different from mine.

However, we all have the same goal: we want to do something with our lives and make the most of every moment we have. We will also face the same basic challenges as everyone else who has travelled this path. You will be reading a number of those stories in the pages to come.

There are two terms that you'll come across frequently in the pages of this book that describes this journey: "The Midlife Launch" and "Lifestyle Business." The question you may have at this moment is what is a Midlife Launch or a Lifestyle Business?

The Midlife Launch is that moment when you have identified your passion and with the possible help of a coach or simply on your own, decide to step out and follow your passion. It is the launching stage of your dream.

Lifestyle Business is building a business centered around what you love to do - your passion, by monetizing it. It is the means by which you'll provide value for others who are willing to pay for it. This becomes the way you'll provide financially for yourself and those you are responsible for. It will not feel like work because you are doing what you love to do in the first place.

Whenever you are considering having a midlife launch, it means that you are tired of doing the same old thing. You are experiencing a mindset shift where the traditional path of work - doing a 9 to 5, having someone else determine your overall welfare, staying in the cubicle or workplace setting until retirement or being fired - doesn't fit you anymore. You want to be unemployable. You no longer want a J.O.B. You don't want to spend the rest of your life trading hours for dollars.

As you may have found out or will find out, this is a major mindset shift especially if you're like me, grew up with this model of 9 to 5; it's all we knew.

There are challenges to overcome when you embark upon this journey.

So, what are some of the common challenges that you will face while pursuing your midlife dream; your passion?

While each individual will face their own challenges that specifically relate to the dream they are pursuing, there are four major challenges that everyone will face, or go through. These challenges if not handled properly, could undermine the success of your dream launch. These challenges are: FEAR, FAMILY, FRIENDS, and RESPONSIBILITIES.

Fear of failure can keep us from trying. Comments from our family and friends, which will be explored in a later chapter, can either discourage or encourage us – and make us feel like failures for trying to pursue our dream. Last, our responsibilities that we already bear can make us think that there is no way we can join the growing and successful ranks of midlife launchers.

Let's look at an example of what could have been a massive failure for a sixteen-year-old teenage boy who was working in France as a Red Cross ambulance driver during World War II. Instead of putting the normal, safe camouflage on his ambulance he drew and doodled all over it.

Returning from France after the war ended, this young man wanted to start a business in the world of commercial art.

He moved back to Kansas City where his family was living, and started a little company called Laugh-O-Grams. To make some money, he created short animated films for a local business or local businesses.

His dream was to make animated films and shows for the average person's enjoyment.

However, before he could get to the place where his dream could be realized, his company went bankrupt.

Instead of giving up, he decided that he was going to pursue other ideas that he had.

He packed his bags and with only $250 dollars in his pocket, moved to Hollywood, where his brother lived.

His brother welcomed him with open arms. He found his brother to be a huge source of encouragement.

They pooled their resources and borrowed additional funds, to set up their startup business inside their uncle's garage. From there they began to get the word out about what they had to offer.

Soon they received an order for their first cartoon — Alice in Cartoonland. It was the same cartoon that the young man had been working on when his company in Kansas City had failed. It wasn't long after this order that he experienced incredible success that catapulted him to the top of the ladder within the Hollywood society.

This young mans name was Walt Disney. (Walt Disney)

He succeeded because he didn't give up.

If we struggle through the challenges, push through the valleys that threaten to swallow us whole, we will come out stronger on the other side. We will come out victorious. We will reach the highest peak that we are striving for.

Don't let the challenges or the valleys you face, discourage you. Always remember there are steps that you can take to overcome them and like Walt Disney, rise to the highest mountain peaks that you could ever dream of.

## FOUR TIPS TO CATAPULT YOU TO THE TOP

There are four very important tips that you can implement to help catapult yourself up to the peak that you want to reach.

The first is: Always, always, always DREAM! If you don't constantly dream, you will lose your drive.

Secondly, be conscious about your dream. Write it down. Talk about it; just make sure you dream. Remember you have gained incredible life experiences - your professional life experience, parenting experience, marriage experience, other relationship experience, negotiation experience and the list goes on. Make use of them.

Thirdly, develop a strong network of like-minded people: this group of people will encourage and support you in your journey.

Fourthly: Take the plunge. This is the most challenging of all four tips. But you'll need to "Just do it!" More on this in the final chapter.

Another interesting story is that of Harland Sanders. Harland had to cook for his entire family from a very young age. His mother taught him how to cook all kinds of southern dishes, including her variation of fried chicken.

As a teenage boy, Harland Sanders held all sorts of jobs. When he was fifty years old, he started running a gas station. Since his gas station didn't have any place for his patrons to eat, he started cooking homemade southern dishes from his personal kitchen and serving them from his living quarters.

It was the middle of the depression, but Harland did relatively well for himself. Later, Harland also opened a hotel and restaurant – things seemed to really be looking up for him.

Soon, though, with new highways being built, his businesses were no longer thriving. The roads made a bypass away from the route where his business was located. He decided to sell out and retire at the age of sixty.

As time went by he was no longer satisfied with retirement. His social security check was just not enough. Why? It was just over $100 per month. He was also bored.

He decided that he needed to do something else with his life besides sitting in a rocking chair waiting to die. One of his great loves – his great passions – was cooking for other people.

He was an excellent cook, having perfected his fried chicken recipe. That decided it.

A few years later, Harland Sanders was able to open his first Kentucky Fried Chicken restaurant. As they say, the rest is history. (Colonel Sanders; Colonel Harland Sanders)

Like Harland Sanders and Walt Disney, you must find and foster the dream that is inside of you. It might be hidden inside or barely visible, but you must find it. More on how to do this in later chapters.

For now, foster your dreams. Fan the flame. Don't let them die!

To succeed - to have a fulfilling life with no regrets, you must do the thing that you are most passionate about. But you need to start now. Time is of an essence. Each day that goes by is one more day that you fail to get started. Eventually the one-of-these-days become a string of days, which become weeks, then months, then years. Without action, you'll still be right where you are.

The late Zig Zigler used to say, "you don't have to be great to start, but you must start to be great."

So, start.

## Chapter 3

## FEAR CAN BE A FOE OF YOUR MIDLIFE LAUNCH

Someone has said Fear is **F**.alse **E**.vidence **A**.ppearing **R**.eal. I'm not sure who gets credit for this because I have heard it from several sources so I'm going to give credit to Anonymous. If you know who is to be credited, please pass it on to them for me or let me know.

I also heard Jack Canfield co-author of "Chicken Soup For The Soul" say it this way: Fear is **F**.antasizing **E**.xperiences **A**.ppearing **R**.eal.

You have your choice of which one to use.

Jack further states that the fear we have is of our own creation, which is fantasy. This fantasy now becomes our reality.

Case and point: Have you ever had an overwhelming, paralyzing fear of something? Maybe you are an arachnophobe? Ooh, what is that? An arachnophobe is someone who has an unusual fear of spiders or scorpions. I promise this is the only big word you'll find in this book. I just wanted to impress you with that.

By me using that word - arachnophobe - I bet your first thought was, this guy knows big words, is well learnt or is trying to impress. If you had any of the three or all three, I created an impression. This you will need to become comfortable with, because you too will learn along the way how to do this.

This is what entrepreneurs or people living their dream do; they try to impress you or create the perception knowing that perception trumps reality. This is lesson #1: You must create a persona of who you are that may seem larger than life if you are going to be successful at the Midlife Launch. Don't get discouraged; you'll discover how to do that as you turn the pages of this book. So that is one quick lesson. What is it? Perception.

So maybe you're not an arachnophobe, but you might be afraid of heights? So afraid that when you are standing on the edge of a cliff, or a tall building, or even a mountain path with an un-walled cliff, you feel paralyzed. Does your fear grip you so completely that you literally cannot move a muscle or it keeps you stuck?

Let me share a personal story with you – a story of my own personal fear of failure that nearly kept me from my midlife launch.

When I was transitioning from my old, steady, nine to five job, I was afraid to leave the security of the established corporate world. After all, I was leaving a place where I had benefits, a title and a steady income.

So, when I was planning on leaving, after almost 20 years of being an employee, fear gripped me. It was very scary for me to no longer have that security - even though this is imaginary.

How secure is it when you're totally dependent on someone else for your paycheck and benefits? That could change any moment. I was at someone else's mercy. How secure is that?

However, this steady paycheck was something I could almost always expect every two weeks. Now looking back, I'm thinking how much trust I placed in this uncertain working environment. I really didn't think much about it then. As a matter of fact, I just took it for granted and had that expectation ... it would always be there.

Even though I didn't want to admit it, I was worried about my family at this time, not just my job. After all, not only was I compromising my so-called security, but I was potentially compromising the financial security of my family.

This intensified my stress over this decision. I kept asking myself, "What if I didn't get something going in the first six months? What if nothing happened for me? Could I really develop my own successful business?"

I tried to hide my fear and my questions from my family so that they wouldn't worry about our future. Hiding my fear and worry from my family intensified the fear for me – it made me that much more indecisive about stepping out on my own and becoming an entrepreneur.

I wasn't feeling scared about making this decision because I was unprepared. No, I was very prepared; I had thought over this entrepreneurial venture of mine for quite a while.

In fact, I had wanted to step out and enter the entrepreneurial lifestyle for almost a year and a half before I actually made the leap. Each time I meant to break away from my 9 to 5 job, I would feel as if I didn't have the courage to take the great leap into the pool of entrepreneurialism, or I would think that it wasn't the right time to start my adventure.

I would always stop myself with these internal thoughts: "What do you think you are doing? What if you fail? Who do you think you are to do this? Aren't you being a bit irresponsible? Why take this risk, when you already have a good job"?

It was my fear speaking. What delayed me? What made me procrastinate? It was fear.

I have come to realize that it was also the fear of being found out. It's the Imposter Syndrome. What's that? The fear that you may be found out to not be what you're trying to portray yourself to be - an "expert" in your field.

After a year and a half of talking to people – getting counsel from others – I still nearly aborted my decision to launch out on my own because there was no guarantee that I would succeed. I only had one or two clients when I started my counseling practice – I didn't have quite enough clients to make ends meet. By the way, I was fifty-one years of age at this point.

If I failed, what would happen? What would people say or think about me? Would they brand me as a failure forever? Could I ever face anyone again if I failed? What about my family? How in the world could I let them down? How could I explain this failure to anyone?

Fear paralyzes you. Sometimes completely. If you let fear enter your heart - your subconscious and conscious mind - it will kill your dreams.

Have you seen a plant die because it wasn't watered? Your dream is a delicate flower that must be nurtured and watered until it becomes a robust and hardy plant that can withstand almost any weather condition and withstand any amount of buffeting.

When fear enters your thoughts and your subconscious, it stifles and kills your dreams just like a drought or a blight will kill a rose bush.

How fearful would you be if you were in business and end up losing thirty-five thousand dollars? What about losing three hundred and fifty thousand dollars? What about losing $35 million? How would you feel? Wouldn't that be one of the most devastating feelings of any that you could have?

If you said yes, you are just like me. I would be totally devastated. To think of all that money gone because of a business failure is something that I have a very difficult time fathoming. I can't comprehend it.

Here are some possible fears that would overcome me. See if any of them resonate with you.

My fears:

- ✓ A ruined reputation: Who would want to be around me and identify themselves with me?

- ✓ Loss of trust: Unable to get investor funding again for another entrepreneurial idea. So much for that.

- ✓ Trying again: How could I, after such a magnanimous failure?

- ✓ Failing again: What if I tried and the same thing happened? It is like getting stung by a bee and then fearing bee-stings even more for the rest of your life.

These are just some of the fears that would be wrapping their tentacles around my neck, choking the very life out of me.

Those fear of failure, if you let them overwhelm you and become a real and tangible part of your psyche, will block you from ever trying to be a success again.

However, not everyone would be as devastated as you and I would be. Yes, it is a huge blow for them, but they would try and find a way to get up and believe that if they were able to do it once, they could do it again.

Welcome to the world of Steve Blank.

In 1993 he founded a company which he called Rocket Science Games. This company, with his innovation, was supposed to revolutionize the gaming industry.

Instead, his company did a belly flop in 1997 – just four years after Blank had founded it. He lost his investors $35 million. $35 million!

However, he didn't give up. No, he didn't even let the fear of failing again paralyze him.

Of course, Blank was not a newcomer to the world of startups and entrepreneurialism. He had already created five other companies. Still, at the age of 44, he could have thrown in the towel and said that start-ups and entrepreneurialism were for young idealists. He was too old for this.

Steve Blank didn't throw in the towel. He didn't give up. Instead, Blank went to work on creating his seventh – and final – company. This company he called E.piphany, which was a customer relations management business.

This company did so well that Blank was able to retire in 1999, just three years after he co-founded E.piphany. Six years later, in 2005, SSA Global Technologies bought E.piphany for $329 million!

He succeeded!

He succeeded in a very big way. However, he could have missed this incredible success, this wealth and this accomplishment, if he had given into fear.

Now, Steve Blank is a published author with several books about his experience as an entrepreneur, an academic lecturer on entrepreneurship with universities such as Stanford and Berkley on his schedule, and a blogger. (Steve Blank)

Steve Blank did not give up – did not give in to his fears, and he has become extremely successful as a result.

## FEAR AND MEDIOCRITY

Fear can keep you rooted to a mediocre way of life. There are three major fears that you and I along with other aspiring entrepreneurs, have to face.

They are the:

1. Fear of failure

2. Fear of loss

3. Fear of rejection

A large number of men and women in midlife tend to hit a wall created by one or more of these fears – a wall unique to this stage of life – that leaves them feeling paralyzed or traumatized. The collision is so traumatic for some that they never recover.

There are others who also hit this wall but are only temporarily stunned by the impact. And then there are some who hit this wall but don't seem fazed by it in the least.

What makes the difference?

Before we answer this question, I want to identify and define the wall that these fears create.

## THE STAGNATION WALL

What is this wall?

This is not a new term. Psychologist Erik Erikson termed this stage of life – the midlife stage – as the stage of stagnation.

This is also what many refer to as the midlife crisis. It becomes a crisis for some because of the impact it has on them. They find themselves caught in trying to figure themselves out. Who am I? What is my purpose? What have I done in my life?

These are just a few of the questions they are trying to answer and in doing so, they find themselves in a blur. So, they make decisions that are mostly emotionally driven, which most often is never the best decisions.

This stagnation also comes because people at this stage more or less know or thought they knew, what they wanted out of life, but now they aren't sure. They are confused.

I was one of those who had hit this wall but didn't know that I did. I did not at the time have an explanation for what was happening to me. This, I believe, happens to a large percentage of men and women in midlife.

This stagnation becomes the breeding ground for a great number of "diseases." I use the word disease to hopefully paint a picture of a health condition.

Some of these diseases are the divorce disease, wanting-to-change-career disease, be-in-the-best-shape-of-life disease, youthful-looking disease, hair-replacement disease, wanting-to-become-your-own-boss, etc. Some of these are just itches and do not become full blown.

I'm not suggesting that these are necessarily bad, so please don't hear that sentiment in what I am saying. It's just what tends to happen to a lot of people at this stage. Again, I too had this disease until I made the decision to get help and beat it.

During this period of midlife crisis, midlife stagnation, midlife career upheaval or simply midlife change, you end up losing more than what you gain unless you decide to make the necessary lifestyle changes. These changes will lead to a healthier lifestyle.

I believe, before you can get into a position to become healthy (physically and mentally) and to overcome stagnation in your career decisions, you must explore the three fears listed below.

Here are the three biggest fears that cause men and women in midlife to stagnate when it comes to career decisions:

**1. Fear of failure** - this fear is huge. It was huge for me as well. I didn't want to fail at what I did, especially since I had a family to support. At least I had a steady income – not guaranteed – but steady.

But what good is a steady income if you are miserable where you are? What good is a steady income if you are "dying" because of your "disease?" Stop fearing failure. Embrace learning experiences (which sometimes come in the form of a seeming failure) and continue to grow. Chase after your dreams with no holds barred. Think of Steve Bank.

**2. Fear of loss** – this fear is a monster. Why? Most of your adult life is wrapped up in what you have done – your accomplishments. You have worked hard to secure them. This is all you know. This is who you are. Take this away and you no longer have an identity.

Here are a few questions that you and I must use to confront this fear: What if you were laid off or fired? What if the company that you currently work for ceased to exist?

So here again is another reframe: What if you were to look at this fear as an opportunity to redefine who you are without what you do – to find your purpose?

I believe this reframe will change the way you look at this fear.

**3. Fear of rejection** - this fear is somewhat similar to the one above. It is found in the loss-corner. Rejection is not something that is easy to handle. We are hesitant to attempt something new if there is risk involved and the chance of success isn't high. This fear can be paralyzing.

The message associated with rejection is that you are no longer loved or accepted. Holding on to what you currently have is safer. This is where the phrase "good becoming the enemy of the best" comes in. That is what is happening here.

So, what if you were to consider this fact: If you are being rejected – no longer being loved or accepted – by some people because you don't have the position you once had, do those people really matter? Were they loving you because of you, or because of what you do?

The fear of failure, is one of the greatest fears that you will face as you pursue our midlife launch and building a business around the work you love to do. It can be an overwhelming fear. It is also an extremely influential fear, tearing down and destroying you after it immobilizes you.

If you recall my story, in the year and a half before my midlife launch and started building my lifestyle business, I was operating from a basis of fear. I was also operating on the assumption that I was most likely to fail in my venture.

This is an excellent example of the power of fear. Not only does fear – especially the fear of failure – paralyze you, it also snowballs into a spirit of negativity. It overwhelms any pocket of positivity that it can find.

Look at it this way: the more you dwell on your fear of failure, the more convinced you become that you <u>will</u> fail. The fear of failure is like a seed. Once you begin to dwell on it, it takes on a life of it's own. It germinates rapidly and grows into actual failure.

You must eradicate and overcome fear to have success!

I will freely admit to you: fear is a part of the process of embracing the Midlife Launch. It is an obstacle that you cannot entirely avoid.

Think of fear like a termite. Termites undermine your house by eating away at the wood structure that you cannot see beneath all the drywall and paint.

However, if you become conscious of the termite problem early enough, you can contact an exterminator and kill all the termites that are attacking your house thereby eradicating the problem. Does this mean the termites will never come back? No. They could at some point in the future. So it is with fear. Once you have identified it as an obstacle to your midlife launch, you can overcome it.

You cannot avoid fear, but you can normalize it.

Normalizing fear does not mean eradicating it completely. As I explained earlier, fear is a natural part of life. We are always going to feel fear in relation to something, whether it is fear of heights, or fear of the dark or fear of spiders. Even though we cannot totally get rid of them, we can prevent them from ruling over us.

I know that the phrase "the power of positive thinking" has gotten a slightly bad rap in some circles. However, this is the cure for fear. Not a complete cure – as I have said, but the way to keep fear from controlling your life.

Take, for example, a person who is afraid of the dark. If they think about happy and lovely and beautiful things as it starts to get dark – if they watch comedies rather than thrillers or murder mysteries – they will be less scared once it is dark both outside the house and within.

So, let's take this example and apply it to the entrepreneurial lifestyle. If you think about success, if you read stories about people who "win" it's more likely you will succeed. You are what you put into your mind.

Negative emotions of all sorts – ones that are slightly milder than fear, will amount to the fear of failure. They will drag you down. Sometimes they are deep-rooted and you have to dig them out of your past so that you can properly re-bury them.

There are so many issues that we face in life that affect us in one way or another. Sometimes we go through life ignoring many of the emotions that are formed because of past experiences. However, these emotions do remain with us and will hinder us from excelling at or achieving certain goals in our lives. They ultimately can hinder the Midlife Launch.

Many years can pass without us realizing how much these internal issues play a role in how we function from day to day. There comes a time when, almost from no-where, we are "hit" by them and sent into a tail-spin.

Sometimes they come without warning, while at other times we see them coming yet feel that we cannot prevent them.

Midlife tends to be the time when these emotions burst on the scene. It's the time when we are not as consumed with pouring our energies into our small children as we used to be. It's the time when we have completed as much schooling as we usually plan to complete. It's the time when we begin to question our purpose – why are we here? What have I accomplished in my life so far?

The moment these things begin to happen, we embark upon a deeper search and, in so doing, stir up parts of our being that have been buried or ignored for years.

It was after many years of working what I would call a 9-5 job – even though I almost always put in over 50+ hours per week – my children becoming less dependent on us as parents, and having completed as much schooling as I had envisioned at this time, that I began to ask some of the above mentioned questions. The answers were somewhat scary and frightening.

There were lots of unanswered questions. I wanted to do something different but wasn't sure I was ready – or capable even – though all the evidence would say otherwise.

I wanted to transition into the world of entrepreneurship. I wanted to launch. I wanted to be in charge of the remaining years of my life. Was I okay with that and was I able to do that, were two of the questions with which I wrestled.

As I searched deeper, I came to the realization that I had some limiting beliefs. One of the major ones had to do with money.

My upbringing, and the various "messages" I received on this topic, created in me a money blockage. I was often told that "money doesn't grow on trees"; "we can't afford it"; "It's wrong and greedy to want to be wealthy".

These are only a few of the messages I received as a child. The messages might not have been communicated in those exact words, but that was the take-away. Now I had to work through this blockage.

Thank God I have since done that with the help of others namely books, podcasts, coaches, programs and mentors. However, there are many who have not been able to work through their blockages and are dealing with residual effects that are now surfacing at this stage in their lives.

In talking with others who have experienced or are experiencing what I'm describing, I have heard of other emotions that have been stirred. Here are a few:

- Un-forgiveness

- Feeling unloved

- Abandonment

- Negative labels ("won't amount to anything", "stupid", "not good-enough", "dumb ", etc.)

- Feeling insecure

These emotions can surface at other times as well. However, it seems that midlife is the most common time for such resurgence, which can easily lead to feeling stuck, angry and depressed. It's part of the so-called crisis.

If you are experiencing what I just described, I would highly recommend you work through this with a professional therapist or life coach. By the way, I am a Certified Life Coach specializing in areas of this kind. So, if I can be of help, please don't hesitate to reach out to me at www.kingsleygrant.com/coachwithme.

This process can be the catalyst that opens a whole new world to you – a catalyst that will position you for the life that you have always wanted to live. This process – the process of working through your emotional blockages to eradicate your fear of failure — will be the key to open the lock of your successful midlife transition.

I'm on my way. You can be too.

## Chapter 4

# FAMILY CAN BE FOES OF YOUR MIDLIFE LAUNCH

Having your family around you is very important. I can't think of anything more important than this. They are the ones who for the most part, are going to be there for you when others won't.

I know this is more of a general statement because it is not true in every case. Not everyone experiences this, but those are the exceptions.

As important as family members can be, they can also be the very ones who stand in the way of progress especially as you attempt to do something that is outside the framework of life as they know it.

They have an idea of how life should be and how it should look, which have been imposed upon them by the culture in which they live as well as from the traditions of past generations.

This is at times a great hurdle, which we will take time to focus on and try to answer some of the questions surrounding this topic.

A few of the questions that you may have are how do you get them (your family) on your side - to understand and support your dreams? How do you get them to shift away from a mindset that supports the traditional path of life - the crib to the cubicle (the workplace) to the casket (the grave)?

This is the model that you have to overcome: birth --> go to school and get an education --> get more education --> get a job or pursue a career --> work for many years and mostly at the same job --> retire and get some form of government payback such as Social Security or Pension in the United States --> work a part-time job because the assistance is not enough to take care of your expenses --> retire again --> die.

This is very ingrained in some if not most of your family members' mindset. How do you break through that wall?

It's important to revisit some of the learning experiences that family bring to your life and how they prepare you for this moment. We cannot discount this fact, so let's create some context before we look for solution.

If you grew up with brothers and sisters, you have immediate and automatic friends. If you didn't have siblings, this might not be true for you but I believe you are imaginative enough to follow this train of thought.

Granted, it might not have seemed like your siblings were automatic friends at times especially when you were fighting as kids, but there were those fun times you had (and all the trouble that you got into) together.

As an adult, you likely are close or very close now. Your siblings are probably the longest, if not the closest, friends you have. They have been there longer than anyone else.

Unfortunately, this wasn't true in my case. I grew up with five siblings - two brothers and three sisters. We fought and made up and had each other to lean on through good and bad times.

However, as we grew older and became adults, we grew apart. We were not a close-knit family.

For many years, I didn't have much communication with my siblings. I migrated to the United States along with my oldest brother. The others stayed in Jamaica.

I remember years passed without me having any contact with some members of my family. I relied more on friends to get me through some of the most difficult times of my life. We - my siblings and I - were not that close.

Things have changed since then, and we are closer today than we have been in a long time. The death of one of my younger sisters and my parents, have made a huge difference.

In general, family members tend to get you through the hard times. If you just got laid off, if you had an awful day at the office, if you are so sick you almost just want to die, who do you turn to? If you are happily married, you turn to your spouse. If you are not married and your parents are still alive, then you would turn to them.

Family encourages you and helps you through the hard times, and family celebrates with you when things go well.

Sometimes, family isn't always a help. Sometimes your wife, or your husband, or even your parents, have a very different idea for your future than you do.

You have a dream, a dream of being an entrepreneur. A dream of starting out on your own – of making a success of yourself outside of the corporate world. Yet maybe your family believes in the corporate world as I outlined above; the traditional path of life.

They may want you to have a 9-5 job. This for them spells out security, status, a peaceful retirement and continued financial stability for your family.

If they believe that, then they will do everything in their power (if you have a very "involved" family) to set you back on the "straight and narrow path" and convince you that you will fail in your entrepreneurial dreams.

If your family does not believe in you, then they will either inadvertently or intentionally try to discourage you from pursuing your midlife dream-life.

Maybe your family is just indifferent to your ventures. They might be used to the normal 9-5 type of life, but they aren't trying to force it on you. Instead, your spouse takes the view that you can make your own mistakes and live with them, almost like he or she doesn't care.

Without your spouse's support — your families' support — the journey of the midlife launch is extra stressful; it's doubly hard. If your spouse — your family — is actively against you, you will consciously or unconsciously be so stressed and fearful that you will be unable to have the success you're hoping for. Unless, that is, you learn how to filter your family's views and / or prepare them in advance.

I have had the above experience from different angles. Everyone experience may differ but they all have some similarities.

My wife is a laid back person. She isn't out-going like me. She could be labeled somewhat of an introvert. She is more the-behind-the-scene kind of person.

When I was going through this very trying time of deciding on which direction to take with my midlife launch, I knew that I had her approval. I really want to emphasize that. She silently supported me all the way.

There were times, that I just wished for her to be a little bit more vocal. Sometimes I just needed to know – to be reminded – that she supported me and was rooting for me. At times, I will admit, her unintentional silence would become a sore point for me. I felt that I needed to seek out and look elsewhere for advice and feedback.

My then pastor's wife - Marlene (not her real name), loves to learn and brainstorm. She has an entrepreneurial mindset, and she has a love for new ideas and innovation.

I would often seek her out and go to her just to be able to bounce ideas off her. This was not hard because at the time, we worked together. Even though I had an excellent brainstorming companion in Marlene, sometimes I just wished that I could do this with my wife in the same way.

However, it just wasn't her personality and I had to remind myself of this and the fact that I had her support. She even supported me having these sessions with Marlene and would sometimes go with me to her house. It was funny on these occasions when Marlene and I would begin to "brainstorm" around any idea, her husband would say to my wife, "let's leave them to their misery" because he wasn't into what we were discussing.

It was a rather different situation with the rest of my family, which wasn't a super big deal for me.

I'm sharing this because it might be a big deal for you. Even though some of them knew of my intentions, there was hardly any feedback. It was very difficult to gauge their thoughts on my endeavor. I didn't see or hear any enthusiasm so it made me wonder whether or not they were pulling for me.

They were of the traditional type where you go to school and get a job, and follow the pattern I outlined earlier.

When I graduated from college and then went on to get my Master's Degree, it was very evident that I had their support. I was taken to dinner and given cards. I received phone calls congratulating me on my accomplishments. I had no doubt they were happy for me. So I know that they had enthusiasm in them when it came to something that fit what they knew.

I must insert here, that I'm not blaming them. They are a product of their environment and had I not come to another way of looking at life, I too might be doing the very same things. I was doing something that went against the grain of all they knew and understood.

I have found out that family members can turn from being the most wonderful and supportive unit anyone in the midlife launch phase could ask for, to being an extremely discouraging entity if they reject your dreams and ideas. People do not approve of what they do not understand. In other words, people are against what they do not understand.

Think about all the great minds who people said were crazy. Do you remember Galileo?

After he discovered the telescope in the Netherlands and began to perfect it, he started observing the night sky. Galileo's study of the night sky turned up things that he did not expect. The Pope did not expect them either. When the famous scientist found out that the earth revolved around the sun instead of all the planets revolving around the earth, and published his findings, he was not received well.

When the Inquisition insisted that he recant his findings, he refused. This led to the Roman Inquisition forcing Galileo to recant or else. Because of his refusal to recant, they placed him on house arrest for the rest of his life. (Galileo)

People have disliked what they could not understand for centuries.

This was true of one of the most recognizable names and figures in this country. She is even much more famous than most actors or actresses.

Her name is Oprah Winfrey.

If you are familiar with her childhood at all, you will know about her very difficult upbringing.

Oprah was born to a very young, single mother who was working as a maid at the time. Right after Oprah's birth, her young mother moved north for a while, leaving the young girl to live with her grandmother for the first six years.

Oprah and her grandmother – who happened to be very strict – lived in abject and rural poverty. However, despite the struggles of poverty and a strict routine, Oprah's grandmother gave her support and affection.

Oprah's mother came back into her life when she was six years old. She took the little girl away with her to live in an inner-city neighborhood in Milwaukee, Wisconsin.

While her mother did not wish her harm, she was not supportive of her, encouraging to her, or affectionate with her. Being very generous, Oprah explained away her mother's lack of supportive emotion to the long hours that she was working as a maid.

However, the rest of Oprah's family did not just lack support for her. No, they abused her. Starting when Oprah was just eight years old – when she was just an innocent, tender, little child – her uncle, her cousin and a family friend, all molested her. They sexually abused this child. Talk about a lack of support in your life and what some close relatives thinks of you.

Can you imagine your family being so unsupportive – so against you – that they would choose to abuse you and to add insult to injuring - sexually? Her mother did nothing to stop it. Can you imagine what this did to Oprah's innocent mind as she tried to process all this? Her mother's love? What love really is? What about the issue of trust? Who could she trust? The ones that should be her protectors, became her abusers. Instead of her family becoming a wonderful, supportive unit it became a destructive one.

Once Oprah was 13 years old, she couldn't take any more of the abuse. So she did what a large number of children who find themselves in situation like these do; she ran away. Of course, her mother eventually got her back, but thankfully she sent her to live with her father.

Oprah's father was supportive of her desires and her dreams. He placed a strong emphasis on education. It was while she was living with her father that she was able to excel in school, winning a full scholarship to Tennessee State University where she studied communication. The Oprah Winfrey that we know today was about to be born. (Oprah Winfrey)

What we can see from Oprah's story is that a person needs emotional support for their dreams – encouragement is mother's milk to a child's ambition and success.

Getting the approval of a parent, especially that of a father, is so crucial to a child's life. The presence or absence of the feeling that your parent approves of you makes all the difference in the world. It shapes your future. Their approval matters.

Approval doesn't mean that they approve of all that you do or say. After all, approval of everything you do or say would simply be poor parenting, or permissive parenting to be more specific. However, "approval" does mean approving of you for who you are – your uniqueness, talents, abilities, personalities and skills.

Now, the child's uniqueness – his talents, his personalities and his skills – might not fit the parents' expectations for him. Most parents have certain unspoken or spoken expectations that they have placed upon their children. When children fail to measure up or meet those expectations, they hear or see the message, "I don't approve of you".

When this happens, that child sets out on a lifetime quest to gain such approval. They will either use certain behaviors in an attempt to attract such approval, or they may begin to look for approval in any place that they can find it, even if that place will ultimately harm or destroy them.

The sad part is that those disappointed children never seem to find it. They almost always come up feeling empty handed, even when it is obvious that a partner or family member is displaying that approval that they seek. They are still longing for their father's approval – or parent's approval – that was never given. Nothing can take the place of that in the grown child's mind.

That adult child focuses on performing to their utmost as they try to answer that question that is constantly floating around in their head, "Am I okay now? Do you approve of me now?"

This vicious cycle will affect every area in your life. It will make it feel like you can never receive enough approval from your spouse.

In your work, it will make you easily swayed by your family's disapproval or your coworkers' opinions. This longing for approval will keep you from following your dreams and venturing out on your own to follow your entrepreneurial inklings. Putting an end to this vicious cycle has to be a priority so that it will not tamp down your dreams and make them die inside of you.

**Here are three steps to put an end to the approval hunt:**

1. Forgive your father (or the person for who's approval you have been seeking) for what he (they) failed to do. Build a case for this person instead of against him. Argue for why he might not have been able to give you the approval you needed. I have written a book on this topic: ForGIFTness - How to forgive when your mind says yes but your heart says no. It's available on Amazon.com

2. Open the door of the "prison" you have kept him in and release him. Keep the door open or better yet, take it off its hinges and get rid of it.

3. Declare yourself free and begin to act free. Be intentional each day until it becomes a part of who you are.

There was once a young, puny, asthmatic, and often very ill young boy. He was so often ill, and so often found it hard to breathe, that he couldn't go to school.

Being home-schooled in the late 1800s did not happen very often. What this little boy loved to do, more than anything, was to observe and read about the animal kingdom and the wonderful world outside of his home town of New York City.

This young boy's parent's indulged his love of books by giving him access to any type of reading material that he wanted. They also indulged his love of stories of travel, adventures, and history by taking him all over Europe.

Who was this small, asthmatic boy who seemed wholly engrossed in and only interested in academic pleasures?

His name was Theodore "Teddy" Roosevelt.

Yes, the President, who was a cowboy and a rancher who led a volunteer cavalry brigade during the Spanish-American War known as the Rough Riders.

This was the man who led the charge up San Juan Hill in Cuba. This was the man who would rock his rocking chair across the porch repeatedly while he was reading on his front porch because he couldn't sit still. It was this puny, asthmatic boy who became the President of the United States. This is the boy who was shot in the chest, in an assassination attempt on his life, and then proceeded to give his speech for an hour and a half before going to see a doctor.

Are you wondering how the little asthmatic boy could turn into such a robust man? It was because his father believed in him, encouraged him, loved him, and motivated him. Theodore's father had a gym built in their fabulous New York City home. He then encouraged his young son to build himself up physically through the use of monkey bars, through weightlifting, and through boxing.

Theodore Roosevelt transformed his life because his father believed in him. (Theodore Roosevelt)

You cannot control your family. You cannot force them to accept your decisions or approve of your actions.

However, you <u>can</u> recognize this impediment to your midlife launch and lifestyle business pursuit, and take charge of how your family's opinions and lack of support, affect you.

That is what Oprah did.

You must realize that people are both afraid of and do not like what they do not understand. Instead of trying to force other people to understand what you are doing, simply know that what you are doing, is for yourself. You only need your and God's approval. You can feel validation and approval by knowing that you – YOU – have the courage to follow your own dreams. Don't think about success – think about fulfilling a dream. Success follows dream.

## Chapter 5

# FRIENDS CAN BE FOES OF YOUR MIDLIFE LAUNCH

Our good friends are there for us through the good and the bad. Their opinion matters to us. They have helped shaped our lives for a long time, giving us council for many of our major life decisions. We probably listened to our friends much more than we listened to our parents when it came to matters of who to date and who to marry.

Our friends – our really good friends – are time tested. We trust their opinions. We love their companionship and we take into serious consideration what they suggest and recommend.

What if our friends are against us taking the action of stepping out on our own and starting our own business or pursuing our dream? (I use the term "business" loosely, describing what an entrepreneurial business founder, what a small business owner, what a freelance writer, and what a freelance musician does.) What if your friends do not agree with your entrepreneurial endeavors?

Will you let them kill your dream? Will you just give up because they do not agree with your ideas?

This can be somewhat of a dilemma, because in the past, our good friends have proven to have our best interests at heart, as they have given us advice and stood with us in tough times.

Because of this we should take into consideration what they have to say but only to the extent that it is not taking us in a direction that could be harmful for us. This might sound like an oxymoron, because I just mentioned that they have our best interest at heart and now implying that they might mislead us. This might not be intentional on their part, but it can happen.

They can serve as our source of feedback and an alternative way of looking at things. We may not have thought out the best plan to make our dreams come true.

There might be a better way to turn our dreams into our reality. They might be able to help us see what we didn't see before. However, we should not let them kill our DREAMS. No, never.

This requires a balancing act. You don't want to offend them to the point where they no longer want to offer you advice. On the other hand, you don't want to accept all that they say just to keep the friendship.

As a matter of fact, if your friends would be so offended that they pull away from you because you don't accept all they say, then you might want to consider getting some other friends.

I know too well how our friends' response can be encouraging and at times discouraging. They are just like you and I and do not have infinite wisdom. They too make mistakes and do not get it right all the time. They too can be very fickle and just like your family, will reject what they do not understand.

Some of my friends – people who are really good friends of mine – did not agree with me when I wanted to start my own counseling practice. In fact, they were rather silent when I started sharing my thoughts with them.

My ex-boss, in fact, is a very good friend of mine. When I resigned he wasn't really happy about my decision. He thought I wasn't making the best choice – a choice that I would have to live with for the rest of my life.

I have another really good friend who thought I wasn't making the right decision. This, though, was in part because of his personality. He is a much more laid back person than I am. He believed in the 9-5 life where you know what your routine holds and where your life is going. He likes the security of knowing that he has a retirement ahead of him. Of course, I didn't get much support from him. At least verbal.

With a lack of support - the kind I was looking for from my current friends – friends who I happened to be quite close to – I had to pivot in my thought process about my expectations.

I started looking for a new group of friends. These new friends were not for the purpose of replacing my current friends. They would not have the history as we did; given time they may, but not anytime soon.

I recognized that and was okay with it. I needed to have some people who were like-minded and would also over time, have my best interest at heart as well.

This is something that you want to do as well. You are where you are because of what you are currently doing and because of those around you.

Someone have said that you are the average of the five people you hang around.

Take a few minutes and think about that. What are your five friends or acquaintances that you hang around doing that you want to do? Are they aspiring to live out their dream with total abandonment? Are they looking for ways to take their "game" to the next level? What are they doing that tells you that they are?

These are just a few of the questions that you need to really think through and then take stock of your circle of friends.

Doing this is paramount to your success. You will not be able to get to where you want without finding a new network of friends who support you. Your journey along the long road of realizing your midlife dream-life will be very hard if you do not do this. More about this in chapter 9.

Here are some of the things I did to begin the process of mindset shift. I joined a group called Toastmasters.

This group is committed to helping its members develop their leadership and speaking skills. It was made up of business people and other professionals. I also did a lot of reading, and listened to a lot of audiobooks and podcasts. My media – my books and audio – became my "friends." They all had one thing in common. They were inspirational and empowering.

Once you have evaluated what your friends have to say, once you have sorted the good from the bad, then it is time to continue to pursue your dream wisely. Don't let your friends discourage you. Remember that people normally do not approve and seemingly are against, what they do not understand.

You must never, ever let people get you down and discourage you. Now, don't get me wrong, it will happen from time to time. Remember becoming discouraged is a choice. Here is what Eleanor Roosevelt had to say, "No one can make you feel inferior without your consent."

If your spouse starts criticizing you and your work habits, it will get you down and discourage you more than anything else – more than having all the world and your friends against you. Of course, if your friends are against you, that will be very hurtful and discouraging.

With their direct or indirect discouraging actions, you might feel like giving up sometimes. You might feel like giving up on everything and everyone – like nothing is worth the stress and the hurt.

I beg you – I encourage you – I implore you, to set aside a little time when you are feeling like throwing your hands up in the air and giving up for good; set aside just a few minutes, an afternoon or a weekend, and remember why you started this journey.

Do you remember the thrill it gave you to talk to anyone and everyone about your ideas, even if they didn't completely agree with you?

Remember why you are doing what you are doing.

Regain your focus.

Go back to the very beginning. Remember your experiences of working for others in the past. Recall how you became disillusioned, dissatisfied and discouraged with how your life had been unfolding up to that point. Remember the feeling of wanting "something more."

You have already tossed and turned over the idea of a career change but realized that was not what you really wanted to do at this point in your life. You don't want another J.O.B.

You have already decided that working for another fifteen to twenty-five years, clocking into work and being told what, when and how to do certain things, is no longer what you want to do. You want to take charge of your life rather than have someone else doing that for you.

You are tired of being ordered around. Now, you want to take control of your own life.

The days of working a 9 to 5 job for thirty or forty years and imagining that somehow you will retire with a pension and be given a gold watch are over. Those days are behind you. Remember that.

Remember, you no longer can rely on having social security or some form of government assistance, which really is not an assistance – it's the government paying back what they took from you over the all years that you worked. Those days of promise are getting darker and darker.

The horror stories of the government not having enough money to pay out to retirees are leaking out more and more, which has become very chilling.

With opposition facing you, do you still want a lifestyle change instead of just a career change? Pursuing your dream demands a lifestyle change, and I believe that you still want that.

If your current group – or set – of friends is discouraging you and thereby causing difficulties for you with this shift, you should join up with other men and women who are in midlife and are having similar feelings of dissatisfaction as you are. Brainstorm with them about ways to make this shift.

Find other people who are already in the game – who have already chosen to launch their dream at midlife – and ask to join them.

Get to know them – befriend them. You will be surprised to see how many men and women in midlife are doing exactly what it is that I am proposing. I'm one of them. So I know it can be done.

Your friends' opposition to your entrepreneurial dream can actually benefit you. While their opposition hurts and can be discouraging, it will cause you to closely evaluate your dreams and aspirations. Your friends' opposition will give you a "moment of truth" where you will realize that the dream you have been holding onto is either not your true dream for your life and you have another one instead, or that yes, this is your dream and the destiny you picture for yourself.

If, in your "moment of truth," you realize that the dream you now have is truly the dream for your life, then you can whole-heartedly pursue it with a guilt free conscience and an overwhelming sense of joy and accomplishment.

I know that the immediate reactions of your discouraging friends, and maybe the immediate reaction of some little part of your own brain, will be "what if it doesn't work?" My response is this: "What if it does work?"

As you find a "new" set of friends who are Midlife Launchers, or who at least have a launching mindset, you will still want to keep your old tried-and-true friends. After all, even though your old friends might not be encouraging you at the moment, you know that they have always been there for you and that they will probably come around in the end. Remember, you don't want to risk losing them.

As you know already, or are finding out, this journey of pursuing your dream-life requires a shift in mindset and in your philosophy of life.

Here is a tip for you: tell your friends that your life will feel incomplete and you will feel like a failure if you do not at least try to pursue this dream. Everyone can relate to this emotion – this motivator. After all, everyone has the love that they lost, or the job that they wish they had gotten, or the opportunity that they wish that they had taken.

Telling your friends this might not have them automatically rally behind you and support you, but it will certainly help ease them into understanding why you are going after your dream. It will also ease the way for their acceptance, and hopefully their full support, of your decision.

## Chapter 6

# THE RESPONSIBILITY CARD

One of the responses I hear more often than not from those who are feeling conflictual about pursuing their dream life versus staying where they are, is that they have too much responsibility. This is not something to take lightly. It is a huge hurdle for some people and maybe it is for you as well.

Responsibility meets you on the way as you step out the door and breathe in the air of doing something different in life. It demands answers. It wants to know what are you going to do about <u>it</u>'s presence and rightly so.

As a responsible person, you do not take this lightly. As a matter of fact you may choose to put your dream on hold temporarily and sometimes permanently, because of your responsibilities.

Here are some of the areas of responsibilities that makes such demands:

- **Your children:** being there for them; being hands on with them

- **Your spouse:** as with children; being there for them ... helping them with the raising of the children ... spending quality time with them

- **Your work:** giving it the best of yourself ... being loyal to it and showing up everyone it calls

There are other responsibilities that aren't mentioned here, but you get the point. As much as this is true, I want you to think about this: what about your responsibility to use the talents (gifts) you have been given to make the world a better place?

Of course you can accomplish a part of that - using your talents - in how you raise your children. I get that. But I also think that there are countless others who are depending on you to be that agent of change for them. Without you and what you bring to the table, their lives will more than likely remain the same or get worse.

So, just for starters, let us acknowledge that we all have responsibilities. In fact, you probably have a lot of responsibilities. Some are very pressing and weighty, and some do not weigh as heavily on your shoulders. It all depends on whether you are in the early stage of midlife with younger kids or the later stage with older kids.

## THE EARLY STAGE:

At this stage you are trying to balance your dreams and desires with your responsibilities to your children. After all, you are still trying to put them through school and give them the best education possible not to mention spending quality and quantity time with them.

You are also probably working longer hours so that you can put aside money for their college. Maybe you have a daughter and you are contemplating the day she will be old enough to become a wife and leave home. This is a frightening thought for me as a dad of an unmarried young adult daughter.

Not only do you have school expenses, college expenses, and a possible future wedding expense weighing down on your shoulders, you are trying to provide your children with a comfortable lifestyle. You want them to have more than you did as a child. Not to mention their wants: laptops, iPads, a cell phone, designer shoes and clothing and more. They, want the status that comes with name brands, and they will make you feel guilty for not giving it to them.

There is a lot of pressure at this stage to say the least. This pressure adds to the frustration and agitation that you are feeling because you are feeling trapped. You have to count the cost to see if you can justify taking the leap for a midlife launch or simply stay where you are sighing your way through this season.

It's hard. I know because I've been there and that is why one of the options is to do the launch with a scale-down version, which is called "on the side hustle" or "test the idea on the side" while you're still doing your work. This will give you something to look forward to while you continue to do what you have to do at this time.

## THE MIDDLE STAGE:

Are you in the Middle stage of Midlife where you may have one child out of college?

Maybe it's your daughter. Is she engaged? Is she still just dating? You are either planning for a wedding now – and planning to shell out the big bucks for it – or you are looking forward into the future and seeing that you will probably be shelling out the big bucks very soon. The dress of her dreams could easily break the bank. Or at least it will feel like it does. I have a daughter who is at this stage of life as of this writing. She is not yet married but could do so whenever she decides. Scary for me.

Is one of your children still in college?

Then you have tuition fees and college debt that you are picking up for that kid. Possibly you are helping them out with gas and offsite housing.

Then there is the plane, bus or train ticket, if they are in a university far away and want to visit or you want them to visit. Then there are the car payments. The clothing allowance. The summer vacations. And the list goes on.

Maybe you have one child left in high school.

Are you hosting sleepovers? Sending him or her to summer camp? Maybe even funding school trips that take your child overseas (if so, then you are already shelling out a hefty sum just to put them in a fabulous private school) Then, of course, there is still all the food that they consume – teenage boys eats a lot as you might have found out – and the clothes that they go-through so quickly as they grow.

If you are a husband, whether or not you have children at home, you still are responsible for your wife. If you are happily married, then you want to provide the absolute best for her. You want her to live like a queen; you want her to want for nothing.

There is no way in the world you would want to submit her to the hardships of a financial situation that is less than what you are able to provide for her now. You want to give her a lovely house, with enough money to decorate it any way in which she wants.

You also want her to be able to get the clothes she wants, go out with her friends if she wants to and when she wants to, and entertain in the style that she likes. You have stuck together, and you know already that she won't be too frivolous with your money. You trust her, and you want to give her everything that a wife could possibly want; of course within reason.

You desperately want to be able to take time just the two of you and go on vacations together. Then there is a house, with mortgage payments. You both need cars, so there might be car payments. Then there is the gas for the two of you. Plus food, of course. And the list goes on and on and on.

Are you a wife asking "what responsibilities do I have?" You have joint responsibilities with your husband for your children. One thing that you and your husband have in common – one thing that every person, whether married or single, has in common – is family. By family, I mean parents, siblings, grandparents. You also have yourself.

Are your parents getting older? Do you need to take care of them? Do they need extra medical care – maybe, very sadly, assisted living? Or, maybe your parent/parents need in-home care. This would require you to possibly move them into your home and hire someone to help you take care of them.

What about siblings? Is one of your siblings going through a hard time? Do they need a helping hand? Are you there to give them a helping hand? What about your grandparents? Are they doing well? Could they use a little extra help in the form of time or money or both?

Granted, you don't have as many responsibilities if you are single, so this will not be the biggest hindrance to your dreams.

However, we all have responsibilities. We all have our own personal responsibilities that are unique to us. Since, most of us in midlife are either married, or at least have one child, this usually is a great concern for us.

The challenge of responsibility is twofold. It is also tied into all the other discouragements that we have discussed so far. Let me explain.

Responsibility hits you hard twice over.

First, you feel guilty when you think about all your responsibilities if you even remotely believe that you might not be able to fulfill them. You feel that the weight of the world is pressing down on your shoulders, and you certainly do not feel like you're capable of carrying that pressure.

Second, other people remind you of your responsibilities. Not only do you feel the extreme pressure of your responsibilities baring down on you, you probably have at least one other person reminding you of those responsibilities.

It might be a child's innocent comments. Have your teenage daughter said to you, "Dad, not again. Why can't we ever go out to eat?" That would make any parent frustrated – any parent who wants to bring simple pleasures like that to their children would feel they are not a good enough parent.

Maybe your spouse is wanting more.

Is your wife complaining? Is she asking when can she get a new sofa? New flooring? Does your wife want to redecorate, relocate, get a new car, or renovate the house? If you cannot give her those things, you are also going to feel inadequate. Maybe your wife is actually berating you for not providing well enough for her.

Or maybe you are a wife, and it is your husband who is putting pressure on you. Are you trying to take care of the house, make your house a home, take care of children or grandchildren, maybe keep up with pets, while working a full-time job? Is he expecting more from you?

Have you decided to follow your dream just to have your husband remind you that there are bills to pay and that it takes the salary that you both make in order to live in the manner you both enjoy? Does his comments, his requests for you to work faster or more efficiently, make it feel as if you are going to be crushed under the weight of the world?

Possibly a parent or a member of your extended family is reminding you of your responsibilities. Are they asking questions such as, "how can you give up your job and your security? Are you crazy? Don't you know that you have people to support? Don't you know they are depending on you?"

We have looked at how our families can add to the weight of our responsibilities – how they can intensify the guilt of responsibility. Our friends' negative comments can also add to the discouragement we are feeling from our various responsibilities.

What about your friends? Are they asking, "How in the world can you even contemplate quitting your "safe" corporate job in order to pursue your "crazy" dream?" Are they questioning your judgment? Are they suggesting that you are being selfish in your ambition to pursue your passion?

Are your friends making you feel like you have a million more problems and a million more responsibilities than you really do? Do they make you feel guilty as if you're doing something wrong?

If you are feeling any of the above, accept them as a normal reaction to their feedback. However, don't let the weight of your responsibilities, which have been made weightier by your friends or family's comments, get you down.

Regroup. Revisit your why - why you're doing this in the first place. This is where you really need to be sure you're doing this for the right reason. It must be that you know you have to do this.

You must remind yourself this is your way of living out the burning desire in your heart and to do anything less, is to settle and return to the comfortable miserable existence and to guarantee having regrets at the end of your life.

Sometimes the reason that this feedback from your friends and family plays such a significant role, is not so much what they say, but it could be that insidious lurking fear residing within your mind. It is that fear of failure. Fear of feeling like you're an impostor.

Here is the question you need to ask yourself: Are you afraid that you will fail if you pursue your passion? More specifically, are you afraid that you will fail in your responsibilities — the responsibilities that you have towards your family, friends, and yourself?

The skewed view of responsibility can be a huge discouragement — a killer of your dreams. I know. I felt that I was failing in my responsibilities at one point as well. It seemed like the weight of the world was going to suffocate me, all because my responsibilities seemed to be too great — too many.

The year 2008 was a very trying one for me. It was a year where it seemed as if my entire world was caving in. It was very trying to say the least.

At one point I even began to second guess my earlier decision to step out onto the ledge of creating a lifestyle business and jump into the cool pool of my dream. I actually thought that I was being punished by God for past sins. I know, it was a crazy supposition, but it was a crazy time for me.

I had recently resigned from my position as the youth minister at the church I had attended for over twenty-five years.

For twenty-one of those many years of attending this church I had served in the capacity of youth minister, on both a part-time and a full-time basis. I enjoyed what I did and had a great relationship with the other staff members.

As time went by I realized that my passion for youth ministry was waning while the desire to do other things was gaining momentum. It could be that I was getting older, as well, and was not feeling as strong of a connection with the ministry as before, though that wasn't my foremost thought.

With my waning desire in mind, I resigned from my position to launch my own psychotherapy practice in June of 2008.

Six months later – December 12th 2008 – a catastrophe struck.

I was in the hospital undergoing quadruple bypass surgery. I had one massive blockage and three other serious blockages in the arteries to my heart. Literally, I could have died, but it wasn't my time.

I had no insurance at this point, and I did not have a whole lot of savings in the bank. Also, I was the main provider for my family. So, not only was I not making much income in my new business, like I was before my surgery, now I was making no income. That's how it would be for the next few months.

You can certainly believe that my responsibilities were weighing heavily on me.

During this period of time I went through the mental, physical, spiritual and emotional roller coaster as Paul described in the book of Corinthians: pressed on every side, perplexed and knocked down. But I also was able to hold onto the hope I had for the future.

Even though I went through those depressing phases – even though my responsibilities felt so heavy at times it seemed like they could crush me – words like the ones below gave me hope. They should give you hope, too.

We are pressed on every side by troubles, but we are not crushed. We are perplexed, but not driven to despair. We are hunted down, but never abandoned by God. We get knocked down, but we are not destroyed. (2 Corinthians 4:8, 9 NLT)

We will not be destroyed, even though it can seem like everything is pressing down on us like ten tons of iron.

Since then, I have authored and published two books, a teen retreat daily devotional, started a blog and podcast site, and currently writing another book and my practice is growing. What if I had given up or looked at things as they are and not what they could be?

What if YOU give up now? What if you look at things as they seem to be now – dire and discouraging – instead of looking ahead to the future to what you could have?

When you are going through a difficult time – when you are feeling your responsibilities weighing down on you with crushing force – remind yourself of these truths:

1. You are not alone

2. You still have life

3. It ain't over

4. Today is not your tomorrow

So, don't let your responsibilities get you down. Don't let people discourage you, and don't let people make you feel irresponsible for following your dreams. Of course, that is if you are being responsible while following your dreams, which I am sure you are.

Let's look at another example – not one from my life, but one that you might be a little bit more familiar with. Have you heard of a man named Gary Heavin? Maybe you haven't but you have probably heard of his business: Curves.

Gary has a very interesting story. One that reveals he most definitely did feel all of his responsibilities weighing down on him with crushing pressure.

He was a college dropout with a desire to make money, and to make it on his own. Gary wanted to start his own business. He longed to strike out on his own, and he was pretty determined to follow that dream.

Not only was Gary interested in entrepreneurialism, he was also interested in fitness and exercise. These two passions led him to starting his own fitness center in Houston. He achieved a very rare and stimulating peak of success At 25 years of age, he became a millionaire.

Can you imagine that? This would make you feel as if you didn't have any responsibilities that you couldn't take care of.

Then, he ran his business into the ground. At the age of 30. He was bankrupt.

Can you imagine just how much of a failure he must have felt especially since he wasn't able to get back on his feet right away? There were so many responsibilities weighing down on him. He had a wife and children. Then his wife divorced him. She took their children away. Gary then ended up in prison because he failed to pay child support.

Can you imagine how heavy these responsibilities must have felt on his shoulder? Cant you imagine how guilty he must have felt? Can you imagine how these responsibilities could become a hindrance to him starting over; starting a new venture?

Jail seemed to help him get his focus back.

Gary remarried, this time to a woman named Diane. Now, with this new wife, Gary picked up Christian values. He started living his life and running his businesses in a very different manner than before.

Gary Heavin started a new business, this time jointly with his wife. He started Curves. He eventually sold his franchise for millions of dollars.

Gary is also an author. (Gary Heavin)

It took Gary Heavin going to jail to no longer be afraid of his responsibilities – to not let them weigh him down so much that he was immobilized by them.

Don't let your responsibilities immobilize you. Don't let your responsibilities raise the fear of failure inside of you – something that your responsibilities can do; something that will crush your dreams.

Now, of course, the remedy for the weight of responsibilities making your shoulders sag and your feet drag is not reverting to irresponsibility. Throwing off your obligations will not help you pursue your dreams. No, the answer is limiting your obligations and managing your responsibilities.

Do not feel that you are responsible for something that actually falls under someone else's "jurisdiction." This can be really tough. Most of us have been raised to take on every single responsibility that is floating around in the environment around us. It doesn't matter if that responsibility was dropped by someone else: it has been ingrained in us that, as adults, we must step up and take it on. We cannot erase any belief that is so ingrained in us overnight. However, we can take steps to remold our ideas and philosophies.

The first step – the most important step for not letting your responsibilities crush your dreams – is to actually take a really good look at the responsibilities that you call your own. Are they really your responsibilities? Are they actual responsibilities, or are some of them really things you felt obliged to do? Is there anything that you can relinquish?

Once you have figured this out and realize that some of these responsibilities can be relinquished, do so. It will feel awkward because you'll be doing something that you have normalized your life around. But this would be your next important step, which needs to be completed before you can feel "free" to pursue your passion and build a lifestyle business around it or a side business.

Just remember, that while you do have responsibilities and always will, that should never, ever, ever kill your passion or don't let it kill your passion. When you follow your dream you will have so much more energy and so much more enthusiasm for fulfilling your responsibilities.

Following your dream is the responsible thing to do. You are also responsible to those whose life depends on you doing so and it is not only within your family or among your friends as important as those are.

# THE MIDLIFE ADVANTAGE

## Chapter 7

# TAPPING INTO YOUR LIFE'S EXPERIENCE

Okay, now that you are almost there to pull the trigger on the launch, what is your next step?

I want to make you aware of one of your most powerful midlife secret weapon - your experience advantage.

As a person in midlife, you have a huge advantage over those who try to go after there dream at a younger age. While younger adults in their twenties, might be spilling over with energy and bouncing off the walls with ideas, you have life experience that they don't have. Plus, you can still be spilling over with energy and bouncing off the walls with ideas as they are, but you have the experience to add to that.

You might not be convinced.

You probably are thinking, "what experience?" "I only have a liberal art degree" or "I didn't go to college" or "I'm only a stay at home mom" or "I've only held one job since getting out of college" and the list goes on.

Because of this you may feel as if you don't have much life experience because it was all centered around one line of work. Let me help you set the record straight. You do have life experience, and a lot of it!

Let's say that you were a stay-at-home parent. You have so much life experience from raising children.

There is no other profession where you are around such whimsical and demanding "little" people, all the time. You have the experience of being an executive; a CEO. You have the experience of being a time management expert. You have to become a very strategic shopper and planner. So you are a strategic expert.

Maybe you manage the finances. You are a financial expert. You have to be a referee, a coach, a counselor and more for your children. You are into one of the most challenging professions of all time. You do not get to take time off from your profession as most people do. Do I need to say more? Do _you_ have experience?

Or, let's say that you graduated college with a degree that you thought would get you an excellent job, and then you did get an excellent job in the corporate world. Maybe you became a nurse, a doctor, an accountant or a school teacher. For all of your professional life, you have stuck with this one career.

However, you dream of doing something else. Something that is not necessarily intrinsically better, but something that you would enjoy more. Do you feel inadequate? Do you feel as if you cannot rise to the challenge of developing a new career; ff launching on your own to pursue your own midlife dream-life?

Believe me, you are more than capable! You have experience from the people you interact with at work, the skills you've picked up along the way, like making things simpler or easier, or from the services you perform as a nurse, school teacher or even a bus driver.

All these experiences aren't taught, they're caught. This, you have as an advantage.

Do you envy those young startups, whether they are in our recent history – startups such as Facebook, Twitter, Apple, Microsoft – or a coffee shop within your neighborhood owned by a couple of young adults? You don't have to envy them from afar anymore. You can join their ranks and become their leaders. This is because you have as we've established above ... the life experience.

You probably have more formal education than a young entrepreneur, whether that is in the form of college degrees, formal training for a job, or on the job training.

For example, just think about how much more you've learned about painting from actually painting over and over again instead of just taking a class on it. If you have taken an art class and you've painted constantly, just imagine the amazing possibilities for your art.

You have been in more relationships than they – possibly you have even been married and have had children – and you have done so much more than they. Think of all the recreational things that you have done. Do you swim? Water ski? Snow ski? Play tennis? Bike?

You have been developing all kinds of skills every day of your life, and you have been interacting (and learning about) all kinds of people through every activity you perform.

Have you volunteered your time or your resources – money, food, house, etc? Right there is another life experience that will help you to become more successful at your midlife launch. You have learned the importance of helping others, and you have also learned how to help others.

Am I making the point on how much experience you have? I hope you're beginning to realize that you do have most of what it takes to realize your midlife dream-life. Maybe what you really need now, is the confidence and a way to overcome the fear of self-doubt.

Here is another way to look at it.

We have to find something that we are going after at this point in our lives that transcends us. It cannot be a thing or we'll attain that and then what.

Our dream has to transcend us. If it is just all about us – who we are, what we do and what we have, we will be men or women most miserable. It is a boring and unfulfilled life. When we are young it doesn't seem this way. It is all about us. We want it all. We want to be somebody and so we set our efforts towards making that happen.

As time goes by, we begin to look around and wonder if this is all there is to life. Is this it? We go to school and if we are lucky, especially in this environment, we might get a job. We go to work and come home and go to work and come home and go to ... you get the picture. This seems like insanity. There has to be more. What might that be?

Right now, living and working in the 9-5 world, probably seems like life is just one big spin. That is exactly what it is when we do not have more to live for. There is hardly any fulfillment when we live this way. There has to be more. How do we find what more is?

I believe if we can place these three lenses in their appropriate position, we can experience a more fulfilled life. These three lenses help us to see our life experience and envision where it can take us.

The three lenses are:

1. The "In front of us" lens

2. The "behind us" lens

3. The "Beside us" lens

**The lens in front of us** allows us to see the future – the possible legacy we can leave behind; how we can influence the future. It helps us keep life in its proper perspective.

In other words, it is our dream combined with a motivator: the fact that we are here on earth for a short period of time. We will not live forever.

**The lens behind us** helps us to see our past. It helps us to look at our lives as impartially as possible, and it helps us to identify our life experiences. Especially, it helps us to identify those life experiences which will help us along our entrepreneurial journey to realize our midlife dream-life.

**The lens beside us** will help us to see what's around us – it helps us identify our assets and experiences in the present. How can we leverage our strengths and other resources to make sure our dream come true?

Yes, we have the necessary experiences that will help us in our midlife launch. This includes our job, our interactions with our families, our leisure activities, our interactions with our friends, etc.

Now, think of your dream – the dream you have that you long to fulfill. That is the fuel for your passion. Envision it. Capture it in your mind.

Now, I want you to identify what other experiences might help you achieve that dream. The wonderful thing about life experiences is that they are not just in our past, they are in our present too.

Is there some education that might help you along the way? Are there some classes that you can take, or some books that you can read, or some lectures that you can attend to help further the pursuit of your dream? Do you need to get another degree or some type of certification so that you can have your own practice or consulting firm?

Look at it this way: there is a season, for everything. It is so important to know what season you are in. There is a season to plant and a season to harvest. A season to laugh and a season to mourn. A season to build and a season to tear down. A season to purchase and a season to sell. A season to eat and a season to – eat (don't mess with this season, or there's painful consequences.) We need to know what season we are in – we need to know what life experiences are behind us, and what we are collecting right now.

If we fail to recognize the season of life that we are in, we could find ourselves missing out on opportunities. In fact, we could find ourselves underachieving and not realizing the potential of our dreams.

In the state that I currently live – Florida – we have hurricane season. Every year we are warned to prepare for this season by purchasing non-perishable items such as canned food, water, batteries and other basic necessities. We are also told to have shutters to cover the windows and any other exposed glass surface nearby.

Most people, including myself, do not heed these warnings as we should. This is mainly because we have prepared in the past and no major hurricane damage, or any other kind of damage, has occurred. God forbid that one year a damaging hurricane does come into our area. I would be out of luck; I would be covered with black and blue marks from kicking myself so hard. By the way, we did have our house severely damaged during one of our many hurricanes.

Another season – one that so many people miss – is the season of change. We are in a changing world, and so many people are living in a world that has passed them by. They refuse to change with technology and the automation process. For some people, that is because change is scary. For other people, they don't trust change.

Like it or not, change is coming. Things are always changing. Sometimes change just happens – there is nothing we can do about burgeoning technologies, unless we are a part of the technology industry. Sometimes, we must change things – we must change what we are doing, if we are going to make our dreams come true.

It was Zig Ziglar who I heard making this statement: In times of change, learners inherit the earth, while the learned **find** themselves beautifully equipped to deal with **a world that no longer exists**. Don't let that be you.

Solomon illustrates the point this way: "A farmer who is too lazy to plough his fields at the right time will have nothing to harvest." (Proverbs 20:4 GNB)

Position yourself for your harvest. Here are 3 ways to do that:

**1. Keep your eyes open** – be on the lookout for opportunities. Notice what is happening – what is opening up around you. Do you see a field that needs to be plowed? Do you see an avenue where you can change something that will let your dream come true? Ask yourself, "What are others doing that I feel that I should be doing?" Continue collecting life experiences!

**2. Keep your ears open** – listen to others – podcasts, audiobooks and other media of people who are doing what you aren't doing but want to do. Listen. Listen. Listen. Read. Read. Read. Get inspired! Learn from other people's life experiences!

**3. Keep your feet moving** - don't sit still. You may not be doing exactly what you want to do right now, but still do something. Don't stagnate. You don't have to be great to start, but you do have to start to be great. In other words, you do not have to be able to achieve your dream immediately after launch, but you do have to strive towards your dream to be able to achieve it. Put your life experiences to use!

When I decided in 2008 that I was going to pursue my own dream, branch out on my own into the world of entrepreneurialism, and start my own practice as a psychotherapist, I identified a need: I had to get my license in order to practice.

Yes, that was a pretty big need – a pretty big chunk of "experience" that I needed under my belt before I started my own practice.

At this point, I already had my Masters Degree. In order to get my license, I had to take a state board exam.

I went to take my exam after two years of internship. In my first attempt I failed by eleven points. This was a big blow for me. I was really depending on getting my license then and there.

Without my license, it was impossible for me to practice on my own.

So, when I went to take it for a second time, I was a little nervous, and that is putting it mildly. The big question circling around and around in my head was, "Would I pass it?" People who hadn't done as well as myself in school had already passed this exam and gotten their licenses.

When I took it again I failed by one point! One point! Can you believe it? I couldn't believe it at that time. I started second guessing myself. I began to wonder if I did the right thing by resigning my previous job; should I have stayed?

I only had one more chance that year to take the test. It can only be taken three times. Before I could take the test that third and final time, I had to wait another three months. I passed it this time!

This leads me to the next thing I wanted to tell you about life experiences: you are going to be constantly learning during your launching. In other words, not only are you learning now, you will be learning in the future.

While you have incredible life experience that will help you pursue your dreams and start making them come true, you will continue to build up your repertoire of life experiences throughout your journey.

There is another very important point that this personal story of mine shows: sometimes your life experiences has come, and will come, in the form of failure or disappointment. Don't let that failure or disappointment discourage you! Don't let it get you down and make you afraid to try again! No, instead, learn from it! After all, learning from our mistakes is a huge part of any and all of our life experiences.

Let me give you another example from my life – an example that shows how life experiences during my entrepreneurial journey helped to refine and better shape how I made my dream come true.

One of my online pursuits – one of the online aspects of my business – is blogging and creating podcast (online radio). At first, when I started blogging and podcasting, I was all over the place trying to decide what I should say or write about. I didn't have any passion to write about – my passion was my psychotherapy practice.

However, even without identifying a subject to write that I was passionate about, my venture started off well. I was doing a commentary about the news on teenage issues and parenting.

After a while, though that blog folded because I simply could not find the motivation to continue it – I didn't have a passion for it. I set it aside for a while to go ahead and find something that I had passion for. Then I started my current blog. It still was all over the place, and I didn't have much feedback. However, the subject matter was my passion, and that made all the difference!

When I started this current blog of mine (as of this writing), I was investing a lot of effort into it, blogging and podcasting all the time. Since I didn't have any feedback, I was wondering "what am I doing? Did I make the right decision?"

After all, I didn't even know if people were reading it and getting anything from it! But it didn't matter because it was something I was passionate about.

My experience during my time as a Midlife entrepreneur helped me to better pursue my dream.

Think about your "negative" life experiences in this way: sometimes in life, you have to cut your losses and move on.

It may not seem like a good decision to cut your losses at the time – it may not seem like this has been an excellent learning experience to you but in the long run you will realize that it was the best decision you made. You will realize that you are furthering your dream by letting extraneous things go – things that you are not passionate about.

This happened to me.

I had invested a considerable amount of money in an online radio show. The project seemed very promising at first and, granted, it quite possibly may have ended up fulfilling what the project seemed to promise. However, as time went by, it became a struggle for me. My passion for this project began to dwindle.

Soon, though, I realized that this radio show wasn't really what I had in mind. Actually, this fact became very apparent to me. But I had invested all this money in the project. How could I back out or "waste" it. Naturally, I wanted to at least recoup some of that money through possible sponsorship or selling products.

After much soul searching and prayer I decided to end the show. Once I made this decision, and especially once I acted on it, a huge burden was lifted off my shoulders.

I could have stayed with the show, basing this decision on the huge amount of money that I had invested in the project. All I could think of is, What about the money?

After all, I had already paid to put my show on the air for a year. But I had to decide what was more important – the money or my sanity and overall health. My sanity and my health won out.

I had to realize that focusing my energy into things that fits me – that fulfills my passion, was what I needed to do. I had to also realize that God can turn things around and give me the results I expected or more.

When I think I am losing money by abandoning something I have no passion for, to pursue something I do have passion for, He - God - can help me recoup my loss through the outcome of the projects that I DO have passion for.

Did I fail, by pulling out of my radio show? No, no, no ... this was a moment of education. I learned something.

This also happened to king Amaziah. He had a similar "What about ..." question. Here's the account:

Amaziah asked the man of God, "But what about all that silver I paid to hire the army of Israel?" The man of God replied, "The Lord is able to give you much more than this!" (2 Chronicles 25:9 NLT). This is the reply that I need to keep in mind.

Therefore, to be able to cut your losses, you need to remember that:

- You have not failed but have rather learned a valuable lesson.

- God is guiding your life and will help you find that which fits you – he has now given you a message out of the "mess."

- Your overall health, and your overall dream, is more valuable than that which you are "losing".

There is another very important thing that your life experience has given you: the knowledge of your strengths and weaknesses. Oh, I am certain that there is a lot more for you to find out. After all, there are so many things left in life for all of us that we have not tried yet.

However, your life experience will have shown you at least a few things by now that you really should not do again ... and some things at which you can excel.

Think about this example: you want to own your own coffee shop. You even have an excellent business sense, funds to start the shop, and you are a connoisseur of coffee.

However, you cannot bake to save your life, and you have tried and tried and tried. Therefore, stick with the business and the coffee side of your coffee shop. Collaborate with someone else for the baked goods side.

Have you enjoyed dabbling in a part of your dream for a while, maybe as a hobby? For example, you want to be a writer. You have kept a journal for years, so you know that you can write. More specifically, you know that you can write about actual events. This might prompt you to try creative writing, to take classes in journalism, or to publish your journals (if you have had an exciting, and maybe public, life).

Let me share the story of a slightly more famous person than myself (not that I consider myself famous) – a person who drew on his life experiences to successfully establish his own business empire.

You actually might not be very familiar with the man himself, but you will certainly be familiar with the creation ... Red Bull.

Red Bull's creator is an Austrian by the name of Dietrich Mateschitz. Dietrich took ten years to graduate from university.

Once he did graduate, he walked away with his marketing degree. Right out of college he did not get his dream job. However, he did get a job – many successive jobs – in a field he was excellent in. He had jobs in the field of marketing.

Dietrich's first job out of college was with a firm called Unilever, where he worked at marketing laundry detergents.

Later he moved on to a company called Blendax – which is a German cosmetic company – where he marketed toothpaste. That certainly doesn't sound very fulfilling does it? Marketing toothpaste? At least Blendax had Dietrich marketing a few other products. They also had him traveling the world.

It was during this time – during Dietrich's stint with Blendax – when he stumbled on the discovery that was to be his success. He stumbled upon a drink called Krating Daeng. This was the drink that he, along with his father and son Thai partners, would transform into Red Bull.

The average person could have supposed that the young Dietrich did not have much direction. They could have assumed that he would certainly not be a very successful man, let alone a very wealthy one.

However, Dietrich was not sitting still. He was developing – amassing – an impressive repertoire of life experiences.

Dietrich Mateschitz was becoming a marketing genius.

When he found a concept he liked, he applied his extensive experience in marketing to make his product a success.

In 1984 he started running with his concept. Thirty years later, he is worth roughly $5.3 billion.

So, what life experiences do you have? Think about all the experiences you've had since you began your adulthood life.

As you look back, you might be seeing the good, the bad and the ugly. All of those are experiences that you can cull through and find the ones where you exemplified much wisdom, strength and ingenuity. Those are what you can export and use for this life that we have been talking about - your midlife dream-life.

You have a wealth of life experience – a stockpile that no young entrepreneur has. So, the question is, what are you going to do with that "wealth?" Let me help you with your answer: You are going to invest it in your dream but in a way where you do not risk everything.

## Chapter 8

## YOUR NETWORK - YOUR NETWORTH

You might have heard the statement, your network equals your net worth. You might have also heard that you are the average of the five people with whom you hang around; those you spend most of your time with.

Imagine that you are a young child again and that you are on the school soccer team, basketball team, or football team – any kind of sports team will work. Then imagine that the ball has been passed to you and is now in your possession for a very brief moment.

You are very aware that you need to get the ball to the other end of the field or court – or you need to hit the ball out of the park. Think about the excitement and the adrenalin of the game. Now, take a deep breath. Imagine two scenarios with me.

**Scenario 1:**

First, I want you to imagine that no one is cheering for you. Not even your team mates. Absolutely no one is collaborating with you or telling you that you can do it, that you can make it.

There are no cheerleaders, there are no noisy fans, and there are no encouraging teammates. In fact, everyone is shouting discouragement at you. Can you imagine that? Can you feel the discouragement seeping into your heart as your muscles tense? Can you feel the blood draining from your vital organs? Can you feel the depressed feelings surfacing?

**Scenario 2:**

Now, go back to seeing yourself with the ball as the game is in full motion. Your next move decides the outcome of the game. To you, in that moment, it feels almost as if life and death hang in the balance. The cheerleaders are cheering and the spectators are screaming. Everyone is encouraging you including your teammates. You know that you are not alone. In fact, you know that everyone is on your side rooting just as hard as they can for you.

In which scenario do you think you are most likely to succeed? In which scenario will you feel the most elation once you succeed? The answer to both is a no-brainer, which I believe you'll agree with me; it's the latter.

You might be asking what does this have to do with the midlife launch. I think everything.

As a midlife-launcher pursuing your dream, you need to develop a network of family, friends and peers that will serve as your support system. You need to develop a network of cheerleaders, brainstorming partners, and loyal fans.

Is your family encouraging? Maybe your wife is behind your endeavors one-hundred percent. That is a wonderful thing. If your wife or your husband can be your biggest fan, you will go far. Is your extended family behind you, cheering you on your way? If they do, you have a built in network of fans already.

What about your current circle of friends? Are they encouraging? Are they supportive? Excellent. You pretty much have your network in place.

My next question is, who can you brainstorm with? Who can encourage you in your launch stage, through every intimate detail? Even if your family and friends are behind you. you still need cheerleaders and "brainstormers" who know what you are going through – who know the terrain of the field on which you are playing.

A ballplayer knows that if they could talk with other ballplayers who have won and lost very close games, they will have a group of like-minded people who get it. They have been there and done that. These are the people he or she would need to sit down with and talk through where they are and where they're going.

How do you build such a network, you might ask? By broadening your horizon. How do you do that?

First, look at your wider circle of acquaintances. Are there any midlife launchers in that circle, some people you just have never taken the time to get close to before? Well then, get to know them or reintroduce yourself.

I can almost positively say that they will be delighted to connect with you. Not only do you want to connect with them, they want to connect with you as well. They want to know what you are doing and how you are doing it. They also want to know about your dreams, and they would love to brainstorm with you.

This helps them as much as it helps you. It helps them to grow and develop new ideas. So, do not fear trying to connect with other launchers who are only in your "acquaintance circle." Those outside will be thrilled to get to know you as well.

While you might have a few – or several – acquaintances who are entrepreneurs, you really need a slightly bigger network of cheerleaders, "brainstormers," and fans. While your acquaintances who have become friends who have become like team members, will be your closest network, you still need a wider network. The broader your network, which is made up of like-minded peers, the greater the experiences and knowledge from which you will have to draw.

Do you remember when you were younger, your parents warning you to not hang around certain kinds of people? Why did they do that? Was it because they thought you were better than them? Maybe some did. But I think the majority of parents warned against hanging around certain types of people because they knew or thought they knew what would happen. They were convinced that you would end up being like them especially if they happened to be the "negative" crowd. Negative because of their behaviors. They didn't want you to become like them.

There is a verse in the Bible that also speaks to this issue. It says, "do not be deceived, evil companionship corrupts good morals." And one of the wisest men that ever lived - Solomon - said, "don't hang around angry people because you will learn their ways."

There is also an old adage that you might remember that says, "birds of a feather flock together" and yet another one that says, "show me your friends and I'll show you who you are."

I believe I've made the point.

Another statement that I've heard that really stuck with me and is very pertinent to this thought, goes something like this: "you are the average of the five people that you hang around." Jim Rohn gets credit for saying this even though it might not have been original with him. He may have made it popular as so many others have done.

I spoke to someone who wants to create a life that they've always wanted. This individual would consider herself to be from the Boomer

Generation. She was born in the early fifties. She told me that she was frustrated with the process because the people she knew, had no clue what it was she was trying to accomplish as she tried to pursue her midlife dream-life. They could not conceive how she could be doing this at her age. In their minds, she should be thinking of living out the rest of her years thinking about retirement, yet here she was trying to create a lifestyle business.

Another frustration for her is when she used terms such as social media, avatar, email automation and other internet related terminology, she was looked upon as if she was an alien. They would look at her with glazed-over eyes. She felt out of place.

Why?

The people that were in her circle, didn't share her vision or her approach to pursuing her dream. As a matter of fact, for them, dreaming was something of the past.

She outgrew her circle in this area and needed to find a new group of people to surround herself with. She needed people who no longer view the traditional model as the only way to do business.

You too might find yourself feeling like she did. You are frustrated and wondering what should you do. How do you go about changing your experience? Where should you start? This might be where you are right now or thinking that no one around you is doing anything close to what you are thinking of doing.

Here are some suggestions as how you might break this "gridlock".

Begin by looking for people in your industry or space where you operate. Do you want to become an independent writer? Then look for the movers and shakers in the writing industry. You are not looking to necessarily sit down with them over coffee even though that is possible, but at this point, it is just getting to know who they are.

You may do this by perusing their websites. Read their blogs, follow them on twitter, go onto their Facebook or LinkedIn pages; look for anything that would give you insight into what they are doing and how they are doing it. They are going to be part of your virtual circle.

This is one of the ways to find out their thought process; how they view life. There are some who are willing to engage with you, while others are constantly looking for ways to give away what they know. They are called influencers.

Here is the key. Don't go looking for someone who is "way up there." The chance of them engaging with you at this point is very low. They are seeking to create circles that are doing what they are doing and more. They too want to keep on learning and also will be the average of the five people they are hanging around.

Therefore, look for others who are following them or are seeking them out and try to engage those individuals. You are more likely to get them wanting to engage with you. Don't see this as settling because for the most part, these individuals are more than likely ahead of you doing things you want to be doing.

Another great way is to listen to the podcasts of people you admire, assuming they do have one. More specifically, listen to podcasts of those who are entrepreneurs in your space or closely related space.

Glean absolutely everything that you can from these people. If they give lectures, or hold seminars or conferences, then do all you can to attend. When you do, engage other attendees as well and if possible, engage the influencers. They are more likely to engage with you because you are at one of their events.

I happen to have gone to a conference and one of the people who I've been admiring from a distance, was going to be a presenter. This person is a huge influencer in the space that I am focusing on. He is not in the exact space, but close enough. He is an author of several books, including a New York Times best seller. He is very well known.

I listened to a podcast of his, and heard him talk about a strategy similar to the one I'm outlining. He shared that one of the ways to engage the influencers who are attending conferences that you will be at, is to invite them to breakfast, lunch or dinner but do so in advance of the conference.

Find a way to make contact with them. Most of them have their contact information available on their website. I researched his information, and contacted his office and was able to make arrangements to have lunch with him. I also did this with the host of the event.

Both of these people accepted my invitation and I was willing to purchase their meals as a token of my appreciation. So, for an hour of their time, I had their full attention and was able to get "free" coaching from them. This hour would have cost me hundreds of dollars if I was to have hired them for a coaching session. This is taking the online engagement, offline.

This is not something that you'll be able to do all the time. As a matter of fact, I'm suggesting this as a supplementary way of networking with those who you admire and desire to be like.

This virtual networking works great, but if you can find similar like-minded people with whom you can meet locally, I believe it might be more advantageous. On the other hand, I've seen where the virtual group seems to get more done because they do not spend a whole lot of time engaged in too much small talk. It's more about an agenda driven meeting. This suits some people. The bottom line is, find what works for you.

If you are unable to find a group that suits you, why not start one. You could engage people online through the several platforms mentioned previously, and invite them to be a part of a virtual group assuming that you have no problem with online groups.

Invite these people, after having built a relationship with them of course, to join you in this group you are putting together.

Explain what it is you are planning to do and how this will be beneficial to them. It's okay to let them know that you are not an expert on facilitating groups like this, but you are willing to host the group. You might be saying, this sounds like a lot of work. It really doesn't have to be.

Your task would simply be making sure everyone gets a chance to share what they are working on, breakthroughs they're having, what they need some help with and what goals they have.

Each person will take turns sharing and then receiving feedback from the other members. It's really a supporting group; a mastermind or a brainstorming group.

It's amazing to see how many people are willing to do this. They too might be looking for ways to do something similar. You just happen to be the one that brought the idea up. You confirmed what they have been thinking and wanting to do.

What's a mastermind group?

It's simply a group of like-minded people who gather together to discuss issues they have in common and to hold each other accountable and to make sure each is progressing in the area they have outlined.

In these groups, people will share what's working for them, what they are working on, success or failures they're experiencing, what future goals they have and ask for help from the other group members. This is one of the main ideas behind a mastermind group.

One of the groups I'm in as of this writing, is made up of other guys who are in different parts of the world. We decided on a time to meet online via Skype and at that time we all get online and share with one another. We first worked out a time that would be good, not perfect but good enough, for everyone involved. For me it's 7a.m EST. For another it is 8a.m CT. For another it's 2pm in the UK, and another, it's 6a.m.

As you can see, it does require some adjustment in your schedule and possibly some sacrifice. The question that drove this for me is, how much is it worth to me? You will have to answer this question as well.

You might not be someone who cares for Virtual groups serving as a mastermind group. I get it. You don't have to. You can do the same where you live.

Obviously, this will only be opened to people who are in close proximity to where you live. You want to avoid people having to drive too far to meet. If they have to do so, the group won't last very long. It's like people who join a gym and have to travel a great distance to get to the gym.

Studies after studies have shown that people give up on going to the gym after a few visits, simply because they have to travel too far to get there. As it is, some who live close by, stop attending after a few weeks.

So how do you go about doing this?

One of the ways is to look around in your community for others who are doing something similar to you. It doesn't have to be related to the same field. In my virtual group, we have an attorney, a sales person, a psychotherapist and a retired military serviceman.

As you can see, we all have different areas of expertise, yet we have this one thing in common ... we want to become entrepreneurs creating our own lifestyle business. So, you could look for people who have that one thing in common.

Once you have identified a few people, I would suggest no more than 5 – 7, then invite them one at a time out to coffee, send them an email, make a phone call or stop by their place of work. Share with them what it is you're trying to do and let them know how you think they would be an asset to this group.

Another popular way is using LinkedIn - an online social media platform, to meet people and then do the very same thing above. Obviously you are looking for people who live within your community.

One of the most popular online sites that is being used to accomplish meeting up with people who are like-minded, is a site by a similar name. It's called meetup.com. At this site you are able to set up your profile showing your area of interest and your location and you will be sent groups that have already been formed that fits what you are looking for. You will have to screen and see which sounds more appealing to you.

Once you have identified a few, the next step is to attend one of their meetings. See what goes on there. If it fits what it is you're looking for, then voila, you've found your group. If you don't then simply go to the next one.

A better way is to set up your own group, which you can do, and invite people to join. This way, you'll know exactly the type of people you'll have there and you will be able to set the agenda for the meetings.

These are just some suggestions as how to build a network of people who will act as your cheerleaders and your fans. They'll be that support group for you. You will no longer have to be in the game alone. You'll have the crowd roar as they see you taking the midlife launch ball down the field.

# THE MIDLIFE LAUNCH

## Chapter 9

# ROB THE GRAVEYARD OF ANY FUTURE RICHES

Always, always, always dream! This phrase is analogous to Sir Winston Churchill's famous speech that inspired a nation at a time that they were possibly doubting the outcome of a war. His words, which are embedded in the annals of history were: Never give up! Never give up! Never, never, never give up!

And so I open this chapter by repeating this phrase: Always be dreaming! Always be dreaming! Always, always, always be dreaming! How does that sound? It might not ring with the booming sound coming from an orator as Churchill, but I hope it's having a similar impact on you as you begin this chapter.

As a matter of fact, if you don't remember anything from this chapter or from this book for that matter, make sure you remember these words: Always be dreaming! Always be dreaming! Always, always, always be dreaming!

I can't emphasize it enough. Keeping your dreams alive and developing new dreams, are like a mother's milk to her newborn baby.

So far, we have discussed the big issues that can sabotage your midlife launch – the things that can kill and destroy your dreams and bury them. We have looked at how fear, family, friends and responsibilities could become the "killers" of your dreams and shared ways to navigate around them.

In this chapter, you will discover another way to protect your dream and why you will want to do so. It's all about keeping the dream alive and not letting it die within you thereby making the graveyard richer.

As I shared earlier, my mom died with a nurse inside of her. That nurse did not have the opportunity to make a difference in someone's life. I feel one of my life's mission is to prevent people from letting the same happen to them.

This was the take-away that I had after listening to one of my favorite speakers – Dr. Myles Munroe – as he spoke to a group of college graduates.

In his speech he shared that a graveyard is one of the wealthiest places on earth.

He explained that a graveyard was wealthy because there are people who were buried there with songs in them that were never sung, books that were never written, ideas that were never birthed, cures for certain diseases that were never developed, and on and on he went. He did not need to say more. I got the message.

After I heard his speech and the analogy of the graveyard, I decided that I did not want to add to the riches of any graveyard. What about you? I realized then that I had something in me that I wanted to get out. Do you have something within you that you long to act upon, that you long to show to the world?

I wanted to live what I considered to be the best life I could live, and I wanted to start immediately. I felt that time was against me. I was in my mid-forties. I had lived a good portion of my life already and was closing in on the halfway point. Of course none of us really know if we will live out the other half but we cannot focus on that. We have to live now.

I wanted to have my own business; I have since done that. The problem with that is this: it has become another J.O.B.

A lot of people who are going after their dream, are doing what I did; exchanged one job for another. Now, don't get me wrong. You might be doing something that is trading hours for dollars, meaning that if you don't put in the hour, you don't make a dollar and you are quite content and energized by that. If that is what you feel you are called to do and is happy doing so, please be my guest. Don't think that you have to leave where you are as long as you are living your dream doing that.

However, if trading hours for dollars is not what you are energized doing and want to do something else, make sure you are not thinking of another J.O.B.

That is what my practice - my business - became; another J.O.B. I love what I do as a Therapist. Helping people work through their issues and coming up with solutions that bring relief to their "pain", is energizing for me. However, it has its limitations.

If I should go on vacation or God forbid, get sick, I don't get paid. That is one thing about an hour for dollar setting. If you find yourself doing a business like I am, and it is your passion and your dream, then your love for it, makes all the difference. You can eventually put systems in place that would afford you to take time off and still make money.

For example, I know of a Dentist who is in the business of trading hours for dollars. He loves what he does and he is a very good dentist. He has to be at work every day.

However, he has systems in place so that if he is not there, he stills brings in an income. He has a number of dental hygienists, who do the cleanings and other dental work, and he gets the income from their work. He also has hired another dentist who comes in on certain days and also does the same. He then pays them. That works for him. He can get sick or take time off, and still generate an income.

Something else that I wanted to do was to become an author, and I have since written several books. I wanted to become a better speaker so that I could inspire hope in others; I have since given a number of speeches while learning the finer art of speaking through Toastmasters International.

What is it that you are longing to accomplish? Have you been suppressing your dreams, tamping them down inside of you so that you can try to happily float along with the tide? This is average living. This is not living the life you've always wanted. This is settling. I call that, living comfortably miserable.

You might be comfortable where you are because of the predictability and so-called security of a paycheck, but you are miserable or if that's too strong a word, discontented.

Stop hiding your dreams! Stop stuffing them down inside of you, trying to keep them from coming out. You will suffocate them and they will suffocate you.

Dreaming is good. It keeps you alive; it makes you excited to wake up each morning. Don't you want to have a purpose in life, something that makes you smile at six o'clock every morning or whatever time you roll out of bed? Don't you want to no longer have that dreaded feeling on Monday morning? Don't you want to say "thank God it's morning" rather than, "Oh God ... it's morning?"

I know that I want to die having emptied myself of all that God has placed in me. The only way to do that, is explore all the possible options available to me. This is not easy. I know it is not. There are a number of issues that we must work through, some of which we talked about earlier.

Having begun my journey, and at this writing, I'm in the early stages of building a lifestyle business around what I love to do. I'm learning as I go.

Like you, I'm figuring it out and to some degree have figured out how to go about it. I know I want to do a great deal of online business and also of motivational speaking. I'm more than 4 years into this new journey - as of this writing - learning and applying what I learn. I have hired different coaches and mentors to help me along the way. This is my investment and my statement of commitment.

Has it been an easy journey? Certainly not.

Has it been worth it? More than definitely.

What about you? Do you want to enrich the graveyard or rob it of any future riches by doing what it is you love to do and feel you were put on this earth to do?

In the words of Steve Jobs to the CEO of PepsiCo when he was trying to recruit him to join Apple, "Do you want to spend the rest of your life selling sugared water or do you want to change the world?"

Remember, your life is as you choose it to be.

There was a young Polish girl who was born into a very middle class family in Jersey City. Her mother was a school teacher, and her father was a pharmaceutical salesman.

This adorable little girl was the first born child of six. Her family's hard working values paid off. When this little girl – Martha – was just three years old, she and her family moved out of the city and into the suburbs.

They were now, officially, comfortable middle class citizens. Martha's father, Edward Kostyra, expected a lot out of his children. While he was strict and had high expectations, he encouraged his children to find and pursue their dreams. He didn't want his children just getting by – just existing – in a job that they hated; he wanted them to live their lives to the fullest!

While the family was living in the suburbs, Martha's mother taught her how to bake, decorate and sew, and Martha's father taught her all kinds of techniques to make her into an excellent gardener.

Not only did Martha's parents encourage her to find and follow her dreams, they encouraged her to be hard working. They encouraged her to have – and pursue – ambitious dreams.

Martha worked hard. Really hard. She had an A average all through school, which earned her a scholarship to Barnard College in New York City. Of course, since the Kostyras were a middle class family with a lot of children, Martha had to work while she was in school in order to pay her expenses.

She was quite a gorgeous girl, so she took up modeling and succeeded at it. This gave her a taste of fame, one that made her decide that she wanted more.

After graduating college, having studied art, European History, and Architectural History – Martha, who was already married to a law student named Andrew, continued her modeling. She was a very beautiful young woman, which won her a measure of success.

Until 1965...

It was then that Martha and her husband Andrew had a baby girl. Martha decided that she wanted to embrace motherhood with the same fervency and energy as she did everything else in her life. So, she decided to take two years out of her career to stay home with her baby girl.

Once Martha did go back to work, in 1967, she decided to dabble in the stock market. Surprisingly, maybe even to herself, she was quite successful as a stockbroker. Martha pursued this career for six years. It was then that she realized her passion was her family – her home, her daughter, and everything that she could do with the two.

Martha and Andrew purchased an old farmhouse that dated back to 1805. As Martha began to lovingly restore it herself, she again discovered her deep love and passion for the art of home decorating and cooking.

In 1976, just three years after leaving her successful career as a stockbroker to pursue her passion for home and family, Martha started her own catering business in her basement with a longtime friend. It sounds like a small beginning, doesn't it?

However, it was a beginning. She started on the path of pursuing the dream she had always nurtured. Her friend left the catering company soon as she found Martha's work ethics and extreme perfectionism, too much for her.

At this time, Martha also opened her own gourmet food store, where she sold her wonderful and delicious creations as well as kitchen supplies.

Within the space of only ten years, Martha would become a household name worth millions of dollars. You know her as Martha Stewart.

Can you imagine becoming a millionaire within ten years of the start of pursuing your lifelong passion? I know you might be thinking that you don't have ten years to spare. You would like the outcome, but in a more expeditious manner. As you will see in subsequent chapters or have seen from your previous reading, this is much easier today than it was in the 70's and even 80's.

Not only was Martha pursuing her dreams at this time, she was also facing some difficulties.

In 1987 Martha and her husband Andrew separated, and in 1990 they divorced. This means that, while Andrew had to help support their daughter, Martha was responsible for both herself and her daughter's welfare.

She was also the head of a booming food and entertainment empire with the launch of her cooking show. Of course, Martha also had to deal with the emotional ramifications of a divorce. Yet, she didn't give up. No, indeed!

Instead, she poured more passion into her business – into her dream – and became even more successful.

All throughout the '80s, Martha was the author of many magazine articles, newspaper columns, and other such pieces of print about food and entertaining. She also authored several books about food and entertaining, including Martha Stewart's Quick Cooks, Weddings, and The Wedding Planner.

In the '90s, Martha began publishing her own magazine, Martha Stewart Living, of which she was the editor. It was around this time that Martha also branched out into professional gardening and flower arranging – in her books and magazines and TV show – a throw back to when her father taught her the techniques of good gardening.

As we all know, Martha faced other adversities, too. Especially the trading scandal of which she was convicted and sentenced to serve time in jail.

Through it all, Martha never gave up her passion for cooking and entertaining and creating a beautiful environment for herself and her guests. (Martha Stewart)

Do you feel as if you can accomplish anything that you want? Do you think that you can find success if you follow your heart and pursue your dreams? If your answer to those questions is no, then I have another question for you: are you still dreaming?

If you are not dreaming about something constantly – if you do not have something to motivate you – then you will not be able to envision success for yourself. Passion gets you places. Complacency does not.

Now, I want you to look deep down inside yourself. What is it that you are passionate about?

Can you find that long lost dream – that spark for something that you could never quite smother? Maybe it is gardening, or woodworking, or painting, or writing, or conducting youth ministries, or going on a mission trip, or traveling the world taking breath-taking pictures or being the next Martha Stewart. Can you identify it? Can you find that spark? Can you rekindle it?

To make your life worth living and to feel or be successful – you must have a passion that drives you. It must be a passion that consumes you and makes you feel as if you will suffocate if you do not find an outlet for it – that is usually an indication of a true passion.

In your search to place your finger on your passion, you might find that only a flicker remains at this moment. That maybe all you need at this present time. That flicker can be fanned into a burning flame. It won't take long for that to happen because the embers are still smoldering.

The remaining chapter will become the wind that will blow those embers into a combusting chambers or a roaring fire.

Maybe you already have found what you are passionate about. Maybe you are very much in tune with your dreams and desires. If so, I congratulate you. You already have a place from which to launch your dream-life; you already have the foundation upon which your dreams will be built.

Even if you do already know what your dream is – even if you already have identified what you are passionate about and are fanning that passion into a consuming fire – I still encourage you to continue to dream. Never let your dream die, and never let the fire of your passion go out.

Surprisingly, the more you dream – the more you feed off your dream – the more you end up feeding your dream the more your dream and passion grows.

Here are a few things we can learn from Martha Stewart and how she pursued, nurtured and lived out her dreams and built her empire:

- She had a perfectionist spirit (This meant that she knew what she did was good, but she always tried to keep doing better – she never "settled," but instead was always growing.)

- She knew it was perfectly okay to start small and that is just what she did; she started small

- She was always dreaming

- She pursued her dreams, always. She kept pursuing her dreams no matter what, by taking action towards them each day

- She did not doubt herself – when you are dreaming, there is minimal room for self-doubts even when things might not be working out the way planned. Everything is possible (and you must always think that way)

- She did everything with passion – every waking moment of her life reflected this passion; the thrill of success and the thrill of following the path that she loved. It must be that way

You must, must, must DREAM! You also must never judge your dreams, or yourself while you dream. Resist that temptation and the pull. Judgment ruins the spontaneity of dreams. It takes the pleasure out of them as well.

You are capable of so much more than what you think you are capable of.

Judgment keeps you from finding out your potential, and it puts out the flames of passion.

Think about it this way: if you judge your partner, isn't he or she going to start sharing less with you and doing less for you over time? Of course! Your partner will also become much less happy and will tend to fade out of your life. You already know that judgment has no place in a lasting healthy relationship.

Just as judgment will kill a relationship, it will also kill your dreams. Your dream will distance itself from you and simply fade off into the night. It will eventually "divorce" you. All you'll have left are memories.

Did you know that dreaming, and acting on your dreams of realizing your midlife dream-life, could actually be very good for your health as well as enrich the quality of your life?

A published study by Jenni Kulmala, Ph.D., and co-workers from the Gerontology Research Center (GEREC) at the University of Jyväskylä, Finland provides "strong evidence that perceived work related stress in midlife predicts functional limitations and disability later in old age."

This study implies that staying in an environment where your stress levels are constantly elevated could prove hazardous to your future health.

What does this mean for you as you contemplate what you should be doing when it comes to your future? Are you going to stay in your stressful work environment simply because you feel there is nothing else you can do? Are you going to stay in it because you are fearful of taking that leap of faith to do something that you know you would enjoy and find less stressful? To do so, could prove to be hazardous to your health.

This was me as I made that BIG decision in 2008 to pursue building a lifestyle business.

After several years of working in an environment that was highly charged with stress – where my stress levels were constantly much higher than they should be, I knew I needed to do something else where my stress levels would be lowered. I was afraid of taking that step.

I ended up having to undergo a quadruple bypass surgery. I could have died from the blockages that occurred. The fact that my high stress levels were a huge contributor to my poor health, scared me. I knew I had to do something. I could not continue that way.

I do understand what you are feeling, and I also understand the reason for some of your hesitancy.

Striking out on your own is risky. It is trading something that is seemingly safe and secure for something seemingly uncertain. I get it.

However, what are you offering up on the altar of "security" when you refuse to listen to and follow your dream? According to this study, it could very well be your health. And furthermore, how secure is it where you are? What guarantees you'll be working where you are tomorrow?

You are going to pay one way or another – now or later. According to this study, you could very well be one of those who end up on old-age disability, which according to the study, could very well be avoided because it is an end result of persistent high stress levels. You have to decide. What is your health worth to you? What is your future worth to you?

I wish I had listened to my body back then instead of ignoring some of the signs of my failing health. Even though I can't say my ill health was totally a result of the stressful environment I worked in, I can certainly say that my environment was a huge contributing factor.

Maybe you cannot make any immediate changes to your situation. Maybe you have to start pursuing your dreams in small steps (I highly recommend this). If this is all you can do at this time, do so.

This "distraction" could serve as a way to lower your stress because you are doing something you are more passionate about. This small shift can have a corollary effect on your overall physiology. You'll begin to feel better, which in turn reduces feelings of stress.

I've seen this happen on many occasions to people I have coached and counseled and have heard from others who have had similar experiences.

You might be thinking, yeah, but what if it adds more stress to my life. Trust me, it will not. Your neurological system will see to it that you are rewarded with the proper feel-good neurotransmitters which will serve as a neutralizer of your high level stressor - cortisol.

I do hope that you will take time to think this through, and make the decision to focus on lowering your stress levels.

Start by pursuing your dream with small incremental steps. I find that when you are doing the things that you love to do, even though there might be some related stress, it will not be anything like what you are currently experiencing. That is why I'm suggesting that you follow your passion of pursuing your dream.

Here is a side note on passion: following your passion alone may not lead to financial success. It is adding your skills or talent to your passion and making sure there is a market for it, that results in financial returns. This is what I help people to do through my coaching program - taking your passion and finding ways to make it financially meaningful. Here is my formula: P (Passion) + S (Skill) + M (Market) = B (Business).

In talking with a number of men and women in midlife, I have begun to see the need and the importance of living the life you truly love rather than living a life you barely tolerate. The possible consequences of failing to act on your dreams can be devastating.

It's amazing how many women and men in midlife are living "comfortably" miserable lives. I believe that term described me at one point.

Even though I enjoyed what I did in the corporate world, I felt that there was something else within me that I wanted to do. One of the first things that happened is that I realized I needed to be unemployable. By that I mean I needed to be my own boss.

Secondly, I needed to be doing what I felt very passionate about, and third, I needed to be making a living from what I was passionate about. If those three things were aligned, why would I need to be employed by someone else? Hence the word unemployable.

Of course, I had to work through a series of internal conflicts, such as limiting beliefs, fear, doubts, risk-taking and other internal and external issues. What was incredibly helpful for me was to have a supportive wife who believed in me and a few key friends who did as well.

These are necessary ingredients for making changes at any point in your life but especially at the midlife stage of life. They helped me stop judging my dreams.

There were three possible consequences of failing to act that really became game-changers for me. I believe that they will also become a game-changer for you and for anyone who finds him or herself having similar internal conflicts to what I described above.

While there were many other consequences that I discovered of not following my dreams, these were the most eye opening consequences for me. I believe that if you are going to make that move and do what you love to do, want to do and need to do, you must embrace these three consequences – they will motivate you.

**Consequence #1: Enriching the Graveyard**

You will enrich the graveyard if you die with your dream inside of you. I know this might be a morbid subject but it needs to be factored into decisions we make for life. By not singing that song that you wanted to sing, writing that book you wanted to write, starting that business you wanted to start, etc., you will have made the graveyard richer.

My mom added to the graveyard riches, and I know a number of others who have added to those riches as well. If you have a dream that you are not attending to in some way, you will do the same. Don't let your dream die within you.

**Consequence #2: Living the Last Few Years of Your Life Filled With Regrets**

This was one of the recurring thoughts that haunted me as I fast-forwarded my life and wondered if I was going to ask the questions "What if?" or "What would have happened if?"

Yes, there will always be a few things that you will ponder – a time or two you will question your decision – no matter what path in life you choose, and I'm not sure you can get away from that. However, the big questions of life such as "What if I had travelled more, loved more, spend more time with family and friends, etc?" are the ones I wanted to avoid. They are the ones that I am sure you want to avoid, too.

I decided to do reverse engineering, which means looking at what I would be doing differently and see what I can do about it now. I have begun reaching out to and spending more time with friends and families to make sure I do as much as I can to lessen the size and number of my regrets.

**Consequence #3: Not Leaving a Legacy**

You can certainly leave a legacy as a great dad or mom, husband or wife, employee / employer, and so on. However, while these are very important, I am speaking of something else.

Again let me say unequivocally that being a great parent, employee/employer, etc, are important and should be focused on. However, the legacy I am describing has to do with your contribution to the "world" – your world. That place of influence you have. Here is how I look at it: whose life is made better because I was here? That's the legacy I'm referring to.

So, what dreams do you have within you?

What do you long to bring into the world? Can you put it into words, while painting a picture of it in your mind?

Dream!

I can't emphasize this enough! You must dream and never cease to do so.

Your dreams are the foundation of your Midlife Launch and your lifestyle business. So, always, always, always DREAM!

## Chapter 10

# TAKING THE PLUNGE

So far in this journey, you have discovered that:

✓ you can overcome your fears

✓ you can evaluate if your family is for you or against you

✓ your friends' discouragement may have stemmed from jealousy or simply a lack of understanding

✓ responsibility doesn't need to hold you back from following your dream

✓ you can give your dream free range

✓ you have incredible life experiences that will help you make your dream come true

- ✓ you can start developing a network of like-minded people, with whom you can brainstorm and be inspired
- ✓ You can rob the graveyard of future riches and you must

As wonderful and as important as these discoveries are, if you want to truly make your dream come true, you must at some point decide to take the "plunge" and jump into the ocean of the Midlife Launch - the ocean that holds your success.

This ocean awaits you and me. We must make the decision to avail ourselves of it. It patiently awaits us, wondering when we are going to jump in. This jump becomes the door to our success story. Without the "jump," no one can experience success.

Every successful Midlife Launcher has had to make a jump at some point or another. Without it they would not have experienced success. You and I must do likewise if we are ever going to succeed in life.

I came to this conclusion from an experience I had while vacationing with my wife in Jamaica of the West Indies. It happened at a city named Negril, which is on the North Coast region of the country and a forty-five minutes' drive from where we were staying in Montego Bay.

This was part of a tour we had arranged through the all-inclusive resort – Sandals Carlisle – where we stayed.

On this bright, beautiful and sunny day, we made plans for a tour that took us to Negril. As part of the tour we stopped at a place called the

Caves. This stop encompassed listening to Jamaican Reggae music, purchasing jerked chicken, soda pops, alcoholic beverages and the choice to jump from a cliff into the ocean - a 33 feet jump.

Standing on the top of the cliff overlooking the ocean and as far as our eyes could see, the water seemed as blue as the sky with a tinge of green and as clear as glass, with the ripples gently blown by the breeze. It was magnificent.

As we approached the edge of the cliff, which was very safe because of these huge stone barriers that you could lean on to look over into the water, we could see a stairway leading down the cliff. This stairway led to a point that you could have a closer view of the ocean. These steps were carefully and securely placed in carved out sections of the rock.

Only those who felt brave enough, even though it was very safe, would walk down these steps for that closer view. They were the steps that those who decided to take the 33-feet leap, would climb to get back to the top of the cliff. There was also an aluminum type ladder that led out of the water for the "jumpers" to grab onto and pull themselves up onto the steps.

Those of us who decided to take the leap were huddled around our guide who was giving us safety tips and would soon demonstrate to us how to safely jump into the sleeping ocean down below us.

"Okay guys, those who are planning to jump, you might want to get a bit closer," he said.

"Everybody cool? Yeah Mon', everything irie. No problem," were his next words as he transitioned into the instructions.

"Guys, first thing, you need to do is to remove your rings from your fingers. We don't want anyone to lose their finger from the jump" as he smiled and proceeded to tell us that it was for our safety. I took my rings off and handed them to my wife who wasn't going to jump and I know it would be safe with her.

"Okay, when you jump, make sure your hands are held close to your side. Yeah Mon. You don't want to have your hands away from your side."

"Jump straight down. You may pinch your nostrils if you so desire, but keep that hand tightly on top of your chest."

"Everybody okay?"

Now that we realized the "yeah mon" as a term that meant "everything is good." We all responded almost in unison, "Yeah Mon."

"I'm going to jump and you can watch me. Before I jump, you can leave me a tip inside that jar over there," pointing to a plastic type jug sitting on one of the huge rocks.

Most of us obliged, realizing that he was "hustling" and wanted to make a few bucks. He pointed to another section of the cliff about 150 yards away from where we were and proceeded to tell us that was where one of the movies, which I don't remember, was filmed. He also mentioned, they used him to jump off the cliff as an extra or as a stand-in for one of the scenes. He was very proud of his accomplishment.

It was very evident that our guide was in excellent shape. He was very dark skinned and his body was as if it was chiseled out of a rock. His stomach was very well defined to fit his muscular frame. His white shorts contrasted with his dark skin. He was also a very pleasant and trustworthy looking guide.

Walking up to the edge of the cliff, he looked back at us in this very relaxed manner. He had no fear. He was well composed. It was evident that he had done this hundreds of times. Before he took the leap, he asked if anyone wanted to take a picture and if so, they should come a bit closer.

He then proceeded to demonstrate how to do it safely.

Without hesitating, he jumped head first into the water.

His jump was spectacular.

Picture perfect.

Immediately I began to think that there was no way I could do that. He hit that water with his hands straight before him. He was like a human bird in his jump and a like a knife cutting through soft butter as he hit the water.

This was his terrain.

He had made this jump countless numbers of time. "How could I do that?" I thought to myself. Was he asking me to do what he had done, or was he encouraging me to just jump?

There were two people ahead of me. The first guy walked to the ledge of the cliff and hesitated. He thought and thought and thought, and said these eternal words:" I can't do this" and walked back to the starting point. That was not what I needed to hear.

His wife who was next in line, stepped around him as he made his way back. She too walked to the edge of the cliff. She stood there, looked over the edge and began to think about the jump. She hesitated for a few minutes.

Luckily she talked her way into it and ... jumped.

How could he – her husband – not jump now?

Before he could muster up the courage, now that his wife had jumped, and decided to try again and then get cold feet, I decided I was going to jump. I didn't want him to add any more anxiety to my moment.

I was a bit anxious at this point and I certainly didn't need any more added stress. So, I made my way on the area that would lead to the cliff overlooking the water.

I walked up to the edge, looked down into the water, and immediately had a tinge of fear and doubt. What was I thinking? Could I change my mind at this point? Even though these thoughts and emotions happened within seconds, it felt like minutes.

I made up my mind I was going to do it. My wife was looking on with a sense of pride as her incredible hero was about to show them how to do it. How could I let her down? I had to make her feel proud and being as competitive as I am, I couldn't back out now. Too much was at stake.

Without further hesitation I jumped and great was the splash thereof. I was pushed to the surface by the mighty ocean almost as fast as I went down.

I did it!

As I swam to the ladder that extended off the side of the cliff, I was greeted with cheers, warm smiles, and other encouraging words. I think my wife was proud of me as well, or at least simply relieved that I came out alive.

Several people who had not jumped for one reason or another inquired about the experience. Was the water cold? Were you afraid? Did it hurt? I was happy to fill in the answers to their questions. I was successful and could now speak of the experience.

Even though the instructor had done a spectacular dive, head first into the ocean, his experience was in no way different than mine. He went head first and I went feet first, but that was where the difference ended. We both penetrated the mighty ocean. We both were successful.

That is the point of experiencing a successful Midlife Launch. It's not how you jump – what matters is the fact that you DO jump.

So many people get close to the edge of the cliff, look over into the ocean that holds the key to their success and turn away without jumping in. They are now left to look on and ask someone else about their successful jump - how was it? Was the water cold? What did it feel like? Were you fearful? And so on.

Having jumped, I decided I wanted to do a repeat performance. It was much easier the second time around. I did have similar fear and doubts, but they were nowhere as big as the first time.

I'm sure the more I jumped, the easier it would be and the more masterful I would become. I could probably jump in head first if I so desired, just as our instructor did. So it is for a person who desires to have a successful launch. They must jump in. They must take the plunge.

Have you jumped in yet? Are you still on the ledge looking over?

Your success could start today if you just make the decision to jump in.

What's keeping you back? Don't let anything suppress your dream!

I have come to believe that nothing is easy that is worth it. If it is worth it, it's gonna be hard at first. Haven't you found that to be true?

Where I am in life today has not come easy. I have had to pay a great price. To become a licensed psychotherapist didn't come easy. It took time, hard work and a whole lot of moolah — dollars. As of this writing I am still paying off student loans and I still have ways to go. Was it worth it? You bet it was. By the way, if you purchased this book, let me say thank you, because you're helping me pay off my student loan. [Smile]

When I was writing one of my previous books, I had to sacrifice quite a bit — setting aside time to write, learning as much as I could to publish my book -- all that wasn't easy. Was it worth it? You bet it was. I could go and on but I think you understand.

There are other times in my life that I have had to dig deep to keep on going. Sometimes there were huge challenges along the way, but something deep within me pushed me forward reminding me why I am doing the things I am doing; why I am pursuing my dream with such fervency. Digging deep is the key to finishing strong.

Solomon cited the importance of digging deep. Here's his take: Wise words are like deep waters; wisdom flows from the wise like a bubbling brook. (Proverbs 18:4 NLT)

You must plunge off the steep cliff of uncertainty and into the ocean of your dreams. To take that plunge, you must first dig deep - for that deep breath - to calm some of your fears.

I spoke to a mom of two young boys who had just gone skiing for the first time. This was in upstate New York. She shared the excitement on their faces as they journeyed to a small slope. On the way, they stopped at a Deli to get a quick bite before getting to their destination.

Seeing the snow on the ground in small piles, they did what any small boys and even some adults seeing snow for the first time would do – they played with the snow.

They were all smiles and giggles as they threw snowballs at each other and whatever else they could safely throw their snowballs at. You can just imagine the scene and the delight on their faces. You would think they had already arrived at their destination.

Once they arrived at the slopes, they were fitted with skis. Their mom made sure they put on the correct size and that they were bundled up with all the accessories they needed for their first skiing experience. They listened carefully to all the instructions that were given to them by the instructor, and then they listened to another pep talk by their mom.

Having been fitted with skis and with ski poles in hand, off they went. Walking slowly through the snow at the base of the slope, they began to experience what it would feel like to one day eventually become expert skiers. This was the most they did ... have the experience of walking with the skies and slip-and-slide here and there. That was skiing for them.

Here are four lessons about how to jump into the deep waters of our dream we can learn from these boys on the slopes:

**1. You must go to the slopes**

This may sound very basic and almost absurd.

However, some people at the transitioning stage of life get overwhelmed by the big picture — the skiing on the slope — that they overlook this very basic step ... starting at the slope.

What is your slope?

My slope was that I had to go back to school to pursue my Masters Degree. I was forty-seven years of age at the time. I needed to know what it was that I wanted to do and then find out which school offered the program that I desired. That was my slope. Identify yours and then jump in.

**2. You must put on the right size skis**

Having gone to the slope and completed that season of schooling, I had to start building my practice — Marriage & Family Therapy — by charging a very minimal amount. I did a lot of pro-bono (still do some) and gave away my service for a minimal cost. I was trying to see what size ski fitted me.

I realized that I could not treat everyone. I had to narrow down my niche, so to speak, in the therapy field. Today, most of the clients that I see have issues surrounding Marriage & Family. You might say that is a no-brainer since my degree is in Marriage and Family Therapy.

But before you get too excited about what might seem to be a "gotcha" moment, I could easily have focused on mostly individual therapy, family therapy, mental health therapy or pre-marital. That was my general training. So, which is the right ski for you? Remember, you will find this out while you jump in and "swim" around.

### 3. You must start on the small slopes

I think #2 above kind of speaks to this issue. However I must add that my small slope also meant treating clients who did not have any severe issues. I would stay away from those who I would consider beyond my pay-grade at the time because I didn't feel as adequately prepared. I stayed on the small slopes for some time until I felt more confident to go to the bigger slopes.

### 4. You must get comfortable with the skis.

Walking in your new skis gives you an opportunity to get adjusted and to make sure the fit is just right. The last thing you want to do is trying to make adjustments on your skis, while coming down the slope. SIDENOTE: I don't have any idea of what skiing down a slope is like ... yet. I've never done any form of snow skiing before, but I do think I understand the concept.

My getting used to the skis was simply taking steps in my counseling practice, trying to make sure each counsel that I gave or question I asked, resonated with my client. I try to not take another step until I feel that what I shared was understood and that it was understood by them. This was my way of walking around.

Now, there is another tip that I have for you to help you enhance your "jump" - Focus.

Focus is one of the key principles that we hear about very often. We are told to focus on our academics, jobs, the projects on which we are working, our families, our health, and the list goes on and on. Being told to focus in this manner is a very good recommendation – one that is worth following.

However, I have found that it is at times a whole lot more challenging than it sounds. Sometimes it is made to seem that all that is needed is focus - a determination. It requires energy and discipline.

The energy part I definitely have – most of the time – but I must confess that I lack the discipline part the majority of the time. At times I wonder if I have a case of ADHD.

One of my struggles is to remain focused on a project that takes more time than I want to give to it. I like when I can get something done really quickly and feel the reward of completion. I love those times.

When I am faced with a long term project, I can easily be distracted. I fight this a lot. As a matter of fact, I have to be in a constant battle with my tendency to be distracted so that I can accomplish some of the projects that I dream of. I am a creator, so I'm almost always in creative mode. I can easily start something and then a creative idea comes to my mind and I am off running with this brand new idea.

In spite of my lack of focus at times, I do find that when I am in my zone – fully focused – I'm less vulnerable to some temptations. Even when they may come to my mind, I am more able to ignore them and stay on target. What do you do to get into your zone?

The completion rate for me when I am in my focused zone is a lot higher. It also adds to my satisfaction container. I like how the apostle Paul captures this thought in the Bible:

"Pay careful attention to your own work, for then you will get the satisfaction of a job well done, and you won't need to compare yourself to anyone else." (Galatians 6:4 NLT)

I believe this is one of the major keys to a life of success and satisfaction.

**Here are 3 ideas to help you experience satisfaction:**

1. **Find your focus zone** – that place where you can have the least amount of distraction possible

2. **Tell someone your plans** – being held accountable is a sure-fire way of finishing what you start, especially if your accountability partner is someone whom you admire

3. **Take time to celebrate your accomplishment** – having points of celebration along the way is as important as #1

More than anything else – more than any way you can prepare for jumping off of your own personal cliff – you just need to take the jump. It doesn't matter how you jump. It doesn't matter if you take baby steps at first. It matters that you jump.

You must plunge off the steep cliff of uncertainty and into the pool of your dreams.

You've been given the green light to go ahead and the tools to do so ... **without giving up what's most important to you or sabotaging your way of living**.

You've done enough thinking. Now Jump!

YOUR JUMP IS YOUR MIDLIFE LAUNCH!

# ABOUT THE AUTHOR

Who Am I and What Qualifies Me?

I am passionate about you discovering the missing ingredients to your success so that you can launch your midlife dream-life and experience a life of significance and be poised to leave behind your own legacy.

Changing the world one dream at a time, is what I'm about.

I know what it is like to feel stuck and unfulfilled and trying everything possible to make changes to my situation, with little or no success. This is draining and sometimes downright discouraging.

That is why I am here to help you build a lifestyle business or a side-business around the work you love, create a financial future you don't have to stress about and at the same time "rob the graveyard" of additional future riches.

I am a licensed Marriage & Family Therapist, Mindset & Communication Coach, Transformational Speaker, Published Author, Podcaster and Workshop Presenter.

I am a member of the American Association of Christian Counselors, a certified instructor in the DiSC Personality Profiling, PAIRS Foundation, and Parenting with Love & Limits.

"Inspiring people to find hope" is the essence of all I do.

**HAVING READ THIS FAR:**

... and you are in **need of COACHING**, please see my offers at:

www.kingsleygrant.com/coachwithme

OR

**email me at:** coachk@kingsleygrant.com

so we can see if we could work together.

**COMPANION EBOOK:**

I have published a practical step by step eBook available at Amazon.com, which can be found on my website at: www.kingsleygrant.com.

It is called: Passion To Profit: 7 Steps To Turn Your Passion And Skills Into Doing What You've Always Wanted To Do

**Here is the link**: http://bit.ly/7stepsebook

**You can follow me on:**

My website: http://www.kingsleygrant.com/

Twitter: @kingsleygrant

Facebook: https://www.facebook.com/ScoreBigMovement

**Listen to my weekly online on-demand radio podcast:**

www.themidlifelaunch.com/podcast

# BIBLIOGRAPHY

Chapter 1

Jobs, Steve. Quotation #38341 from Classic Quotes. The Quotations Page. Retrieved from http://www.quotationspage.com/quote/38341.html

Chapter 2

Colonel Sanders. Retrieved July 2, 2015 from Wikipedia. https://en.wikipedia.org/wiki/Colonel_Sanders

Colonel Harland Sanders. (2015). The Biography.com website. Retrieved 11:28, Jul 02, 2015, from http://www.biography.com/people/colonel-harland-sanders-12353545.

Walt Disney. Retrieved July 2, 2015 from Wikipedia. https://en.wikipedia.org/wiki/Walt_Disney

Walt Disney. (2015). The Biography.com website. Retrieved 10:54, Jul 02, 2015, from http://www.biography.com/people/walt-disney-9275533.

Chapter 3

Steve Blank. Retrieved July 2, 2015 from Wikipedia. https://en.wikipedia.org/wiki/Steve_Blank

Chapter 4

Galileo. In Encyclopedia Britannica online. Retrieved from http://www.britannica.com/biography/Galileo-Galilei

Oprah Winfrey. (2015). The Biography.com website. Retrieved July 3, 2015, from http://www.biography.com/people/oprah-winfrey-9534419#success-and-fame

Oprah Winfrey. Academy of Achievement.org website. Retrieved from http://www.achievement.org/autodoc/page/win0bio-1

Theodore Roosevelt. The Biography.com website. Retrieved from http://www.biography.com/people/theodore-roosevelt-9463424#synopsis

Theodore Roosevelt. History website. Retrieved from http://www.history.com/topics/us-presidents/theodore-roosevelt

Chapter 6

Gary Heavin. Wikipedia. Retrieved from https://en.wikipedia.org/wiki/Gary_Heavin

Gary Heavin. Bloomberg Business. Retrieved from http://www.bloomberg.com/research/stocks/private/person.asp?personId=23855992&privcapId=4421838&%2520Travel%2520LLC

Chapter 7

Kulmala, Jenni, Ph.D. Are psychosocial symptoms and self rated health early and shared risk factors for physical disability and cognitive decline in old age? Post-Doctoral Research for the University of Jyväskylä, Finland

Martha Stewart. Reference for Business.com. Retrieved from http://www.referenceforbusiness.com/biography/S-Z/Stewart-Martha-1941.html

Chapter 8

Dietrich Mateschitz. Forbes, The World's Billionaires. Retrieved from http://www.forbes.com/profile/dietrich-mateschitz/

Dietrich Mateschitz. Wikipedia. Retrieved from https://en.wikipedia.org/wiki/Dietrich_Mateschitz

www.ingramcontent.com/pod-product-compliance
Lightning Source LLC
LaVergne TN
LVHW051603070426
835507LV00021B/2741